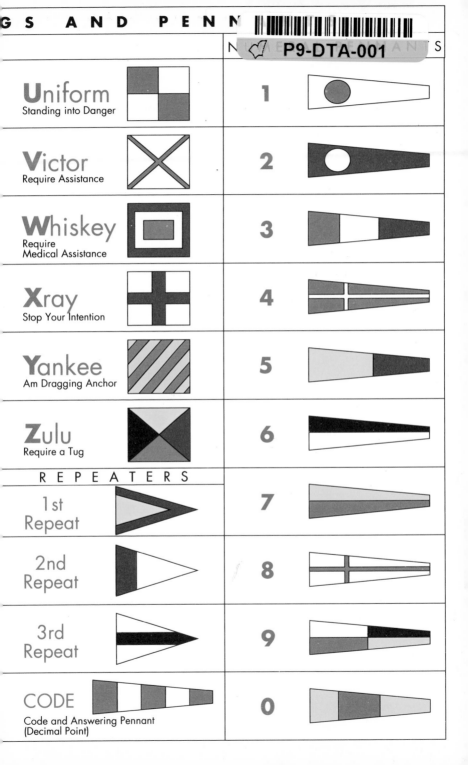

P9-DTA-001

Flag	Meaning		Numeral	
Uniform	Standing into Danger		1	
Victor	Require Assistance		2	
Whiskey	Require Medical Assistance		3	
Xray	Stop Your Intention		4	
Yankee	Am Dragging Anchor		5	
Zulu	Require a Tug		6	

REPEATERS

1st Repeat			7	
2nd Repeat			8	
3rd Repeat			9	
CODE — Code and Answering Pennant (Decimal Point)			0	

Boating Etiquette

CHAPMAN'S
Nautical Guides

Boating Etiquette

by   Queene   Hooper   Foster

HEARST MARINE BOOKS
New York

Library of Congress Catalog Card Number: 89-81526

ISBN: 0-688-09457-0

Printed in Italy
First U.S. Edition
1 2 3 4 5 6 7 8 9 10

Book design by Mary Moriarty
Edited by Lucy A. O'Brien
Produced by Smallwood and Stewart
9 West 19th Street
New York, N.Y. 10011

CONTENTS

CHAPTER ONE

REASONS FOR BOATING ETIQUETTE

B oating etiquette is more than tipping your hat to the commodore. Harbor manners, an important part of this book, are the operational component of boating etiquette and relate directly to safe boat operation in crowded waters. Manners are more important today than they were in the Gilded Age of yachting, because our waters are more congested with a wide variety of watercraft. Good harbor manners are the product of long experience: the skippers with the best manners are those who have been on the water many years. To those mariners, most of what is in this book will seem like common sense, and something they have always known. The boat operators with the worst manners are often those who just wrote out the check at the boat show, and are testing the limits of their new toys on the water. To them, a book on etiquette might seem silly or arbitrary, perhaps a little stuffy in its emphasis on what is polite or proper. But good manners are not the stuff of late-night boasts around the cabin table or sea stories at the yacht club bar; good manners in crowded waters are a true mark of good seamanship and they deserve the highest level of respect and attention from all mariners. There are many books on the topics of storms at sea, emergency repairs, and man-overboard equipment, as there should be, but there has been little written on the safest way to enter a crowded channel, on passing a small boat with the least distress, or on giving up your right-of-way to a larger vessel.

At a time when operator licensing is a topic of much discussion throughout the boating world, we hear little discussion of how one should actually behave on the water, with or without legislation. Good manners are not subject to regulation and have rarely been identified. If everyone who ventured on the water had a better understanding of good manners, which are really a part of good seamanship, then further legislation might be avoided.

Flags, another chapter herein, are often the first identifying marks on a boat, and as in the great age of sail, they are the first thing you can "read" about a vessel. Is she friendly? In distress? Is the owner aboard? Is she well kept-up? Proper flying of flags can communicate a great many things, as the following chapter on flags will show. Incorrect flying of flags is much like graffiti—it communicates nothing, and offends the eye. It also offends anyone who understands the value of communication by flags, and the tradition thereby represented. Observance of "colors" is a way of proclaiming: "Boating is fun, and I know how to play the game." And since flags snapping in the sunlight can be truly beautiful, it is a way for one boat to add to the beauty of the sport with color, tradition, and ceremony.

Ten Rules of Good Boating Etiquette
1. *Scrupulous observance of the Rules of the Road (see chapter 3)*
2. *Common sense at the helm and throttle*
3. *No wake in harbors or near other boats*
4. *Sensible anchoring practice*
5. *Proper disposal of ship's refuse and sewage*
6. *Quiet operation*

7. *Appropriate communications*

8. *Clean topsides and waterline*

9. *Observance of colors (flags)*

10. *Taut ship: i.e., no flapping laundry out to dry, no flapping halyards or other loose lines, no droopy awnings and sail covers, no fenders adangle*

CHAPTER TWO

FLAGS, OR
OBSERVING COLORS

On the huge, reborn J-class yacht *Endeavour*, the burgee is a flag measuring four feet on the hoist and six feet on the fly. It is secured to an aluminum "pig stick" (the masthead flagstaff), which was formerly a sailboard mast, about eighteen feet long and three inches in diameter. When the flag and pole are raised to the masthead on the 330-foot flag halyard, a brave man or woman in a bosun's chair, on another halyard, accompanies the cumbersome apparatus aloft to be sure it clears the masthead instrument array. It must clear four sets of spreaders, six antennae, and two separate sets of running backstays on its way to the top of the 165-foot mast. Furthermore, the wind direction and strength at the masthead may be quite different than on deck, sixteen stories below, complicating the maneuver even more. The captain has been known to spin the 130-foot boat in circles under power, eyes aloft, to the consternation of the spectator fleet always in attendance, just to help the burgee clear the obstacles on its way aloft. It represents a tremendous effort on a daily basis to observe colors and it indicates a great deal

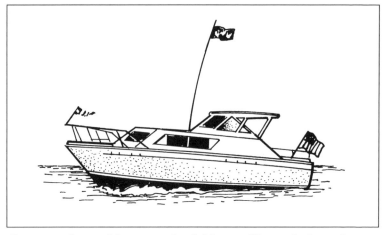

On a powerboat with a mast, the club burgee flies at the bow, the private signal at the masthead, and the ensign on the stern.

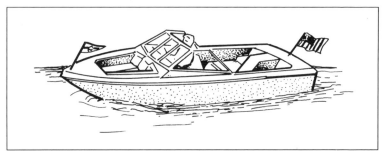

A powerboat with no mast carries the club burgee or the private signal on the bow, and the ensign on the stern.

about that yacht and how she operates. Surely lesser vessels can observe colors without complaining that it's too much work.

Flags constitute a language conveying information to those who speak that language. Before the era of radio, telephones, or Morse code, a vessel could still signal a great deal about her nationality, her owner, and even her intentions to any captain for miles around,

because the language of flags was understood. Since it was vitally important for a captain to know if an approaching vessel was from a friendly nation, in the naval or merchant service, or even a pleasure boat, and useful to know many other things about her, the language of flags became the international language among ships. An explanatory book "intended to cater primarily to situations related to safety of navigation and persons, especially when language difficulties arise" was published by the British Board of Trade in 1897 and

A sloop flies the club burgee or private signal at the masthead, and the ensign on the stern or on the leech of the sail.

distributed to all maritime powers. The 156-page book, *International Code of Signals, H.O. Pub. No. 102,* is still available (revised since the original) to any captain who wishes to say, among other things, "I am abandoning my vessel which has suffered a nuclear accident and is a possible source of radiation danger" (with the two flags, AD). In fact that book, along with a complete set of code flags, is required safety equipment on any yacht competing in the Newport to Bermuda Race. It would permit a yacht to communicate emergency or medical information to Norwegian and Russian ships (presumably standing by) simultaneously, without using either language.

If flags represent the components of a language, their correct placement on the vessel represents the grammar of that language. The right flags flown in the right places and at the right times of day mark the skipper as one who speaks the language of flags. It is not a crime to misuse the language of flags, any more than it is a crime to sing out of tune. But among those who know the difference, it is an unwelcome sight.

Just as there are great debates among language experts about correct word usage, so there are many heated discussions in print and at the dock about correct flag usage. There are rigid schools of thought (the burgee comes down at sunset), and time-honored expediencies (the burgee stays aloft twenty-four hours a day), proponents of new slang (the burgee flies under the starboard spreader), and revisionists (the burgee flies above the bow pulpit on both sail- and powerboats). For the most basic, everyday use, flag etiquette is simple and easy; raise the national flag in the place of honor at 8:00 A.M., take it down at sunset. If you do no more than that you are doing fine. Yacht-club burgees, private signals, Union Jacks, code flags, and pennants are seemingly less well understood, and their location and hours aloft seem to vary, but they are also fairly simple to use correctly, once you decide to set up the necessary halyards and clips and make it a part of your daily shipboard routine. While there are those who might debate the particulars of what is outlined below, it remains the accepted standard of flag etiquette, taken from *Chapman Piloting: Seamanship & Small Boat Handling* (Elbert S. Maloney, Hearst Marine Books), the United States Power Squadrons (USPS), and the New York Yacht Club yearbook.

The United States Ensign

T he flag of the United States, the thirteen stripes and fifty stars, is called the national ensign when it flies at the stern of a vessel. It denotes the nationality of the vessel or of her owner. It is distinct from the yacht ensign, mentioned below, which has the fouled anchor and thirteen stars in place of the fifty stars. Even the skipper who cries bah-humbug to flag etiquette and tradition should know the proper display of the national ensign.

The ensign should be flown from 8 A.M. until sunset when the vessel is in commission, though it may be flown when entering a harbor at night for identification purposes. It should be the first flag raised in the morning, sharply at 8 A.M., when yacht clubs may fire a cannon to waken the fleet, and is followed promptly by other flags, burgees, private signals, and so forth. Not so many years ago, ladies who might be aboard the yacht were not permitted to go on deck before colors, because the gentlemen might be enjoying their morning swim over the side, in the nude. The ensign should be the last flag brought in at sunset, again often to the signal given by clubs or flagships, except on Sunday, when no cannon is fired. It should be hoisted smartly, and brought in ceremoniously.

The national ensign should be flown in the place of honor on the boat. Traditionally the captain's domain, the stern of the vessel is still the place of honor, as is the peak of the raised gaff, if you happen to have a gaff-rigged vessel. Whether on a powerboat or sailboat, the flag should be raised to the peak of the gaff when under way. Marconi-rigged sailboats can fly the flag from the leech of the aftermost sail, about two-thirds of the way up the sail, where the gaff would be if the boat were gaff-rigged. When at anchor or at the dock, or when the sail is doused, the flag should be hoisted at the stern. When the sailboat is actively racing, no flags are shown, except identifying flags specified by the race committee or sponsoring club.

The term "colors" technically applies only to the flag at the stern denoting nationality. In practice, however, it has come to mean all the flags flown, all the snapping banners of color, and their timely display.

Rules for All Ensigns

The size of the ensign is determined by the length of the vessel: one inch on the fly (the longer dimension) for every foot of over-all length. (The ratio between the fly and the hoist is usually 3:2.) That means that for a thirty-nine-foot boat, the flag should be at least thirty-nine inches long. Since standard sizes for flags offer only a thirty-six-inch flag and a forty-eight-inch flag, choose the larger flag; better to err with a flag that's too big than one that's too small. An oversize flag rippling over the water can be a beautiful sight.

Some larger boats prefer to secure the flag to the staff with a tiny halyard, to permit the dipping of colors, and to leave the staff in place, bare, when the flag is lowered. Sailboats with overhanging booms may rig the flag from the boom to the rail, and dispense with the staff entirely. Sportfishing boats, which cannot fly a flag on a stern staff, as it interferes with the fishing lines over the stern, have evolved a practical routine of flying the ensign from the tuna towers.

If some obstacle, such as a boarding ladder or an overhanging boom, should interfere with the centerline placement of the flagstaff, it should be located slightly to starboard of the centerline.

When flown upside down, the national ensign is an unofficial but effective distress signal.

It should hardly be necessary to say: the flag should be kept clean of grease and exhaust fumes, neither torn nor badly frayed, and it should be kept taut along its hoist.

Here are a few more pointers to spare embarrassment to neophytes on the water:

The U.S. flag should never be flown from the starboard flag hoist (under the starboard spreader) unless the vessel is under foreign ownership and is visiting U.S. waters.

If you are leaving the vessel before sunset, for example to go ashore for dinner, and won't return until after colors, take the ensign in before you leave the boat.

Don't fly the ensign from the backstay; while it is handy, the angle of the backstay will not allow the flag to fly freely.

Don't fly your state flag at the stern. It may be flown from the starboard spreader, if you need it.

Don't dry the mop in the bracket for the flagstaff.

The Yacht Ensign

T raditionally, only yachts documented with the federal government could fly the yacht ensign, the one with the red and white stripes and the thirteen stars and fouled anchor. Now, however, any yacht, documented or not, may fly the yacht ensign in domestic waters, in place of and in the manner of the national ensign. Designed in 1848 by the New York Yacht Club at the request of the Secretary of the Navy, it was intended to differentiate yachts from commercial vessels, as they might otherwise look the same in those days. It should not be flown on any yacht in foreign waters, where the stars and stripes is the only recognized national standard.

The Power Squadrons Ensign

T he ensign of the United States Power Squadrons may be displayed only by enrolled members of the USPS. Their flag has blue and white vertical stripes, and the upper left corner (or canton) comprises a red field containing a white fouled anchor encircled by thirteen stars.

The Power Squadrons credo reads: "It is an outward and visible sign that the vessel displaying it is under the charge of a person who has made a study of piloting and small boat handling, and will recognize the rights of others and the traditions of the sea. The Squadrons' Ensign also marks a craft as being under the command of a man or woman who has met certain minimum requirements and is so honored for meeting them."

While its preferred location is under the starboard spreader, the USPS ensign may be flown in place of the national ensign on smaller powerboats without masts.

The Yacht Club Burgee

Y achts enrolled in a yacht club are entitled to fly that club's burgee, except when they are under charter to a nonmember. The burgee (pronounced: "brr, gee it's a cold night") is flown from the forwardmost truck (the tip of the masthead), or, lacking masts, from the bow staff. It is usually a triangular flag and should be a half-inch on the fly for every foot of the tallest mast. Powerboats should fly burgees roughly five-eighths of an inch on the fly for every foot of overall length. It is raised at colors (8 A.M.), when (or soon after) the ensign is raised, and it is lowered at sunset. However, every club has its own routine for flag display, and members should follow their club's guidelines. Members

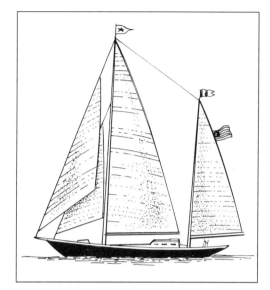

On a yawl or ketch, the club burgee flies at the mainmast head, and the private signal at the mizzen masthead.

of the Cruising Club of America, for example, fly their burgee twenty-four hours a day.

Be careful not to fly your club flag upside down by mistake; if it has a star, that star should point up.

A big problem with the burgee at the masthead is that it interferes with all the new gear that

On a schooner, the private signal is on the mainmast, and the club burgee on the foremast.

sailboats seem to collect at the top of the mast. Antennae and anemometers are delicate instruments, and they sprout right where the burgee should be, flying free above the truck. Such instruments are easily damaged by a whipping burgee with a long stick attached. The trick is that the pig stick must be long enough and light enough to lift the burgee above the instruments when it is raised to the fullest. A wooden dowel or an old broom handle works well, or an aluminum pole for the high-tech yacht. Make it longer than you might think necessary, up to four or five feet long, with most of its length above the knots of the halyard. The flag halyard should go up the starboard side of the mast, and should be cleated at the shrouds or the chainplates, where it will not chatter against the mast in a breeze.

It will take practice to be able to raise the burgee efficiently, plus what may seem like hours of straining your neck and staring into the sun. The worst part is just before the burgee breaks into clear air above the masthead, when it hangs up on the shroud tangs or on the mast crane and seems to want to knock out the antenna. It whips the antenna at high frequency and snarls itself in a knot around it. This is where you curse flag etiquette in general. Then the flag breaks free above the truck, clear of gear and fluttering smartly for all to see. You may be tempted to nail it there and leave it up day and night, once it is up and flying.

Commodore Frank V. Snyder of the New York Yacht Club once said, in exhorting the assembled skippers at the club's annual cruise to observe proper use of the club's flag, "If you don't know where the top of your mast is, don't fly the burgee."

Powerboats have an easier time with burgees; theirs is set on a short bow staff above the bow pulpit, flying freely over the foredeck.

Private Signals

T he private signal (also called the house flag, in the manner of the merchant shipping lines) is a flag designed by the owner to identify his or her vessel. It is flown from the aftermost mast (or the mainmast on vessels with more than two masts), or in place of the club burgee on single-masted vessels. On powerboats with no masts, the private signal may replace the club burgee at the bow staff. It can be triangular, swallow-tailed, rectangular, or pennant-shaped; its size is about the same as a yacht-club burgee. Even though *Lloyd's Register of American Yachts*, which included a register of private signals, no longer exists, private signals are still helpful in distinguishing a yacht from her sisterships at a distance, and in cases of more than one owner, in indicating which partner is aboard. Private signals may give a hint of the owner's name by an initial, a color, or shape. They may be flown by day only, or day and night.

The Union Jack

I f the blue canton with the fifty white stars could be cut out of the yacht's national flag and become a flag itself, it would be the Union Jack. While U.S. naval vessels display the Union Jack at the bow when at anchor, yachts should fly theirs only between 8 A.M. and sunset on Sun-

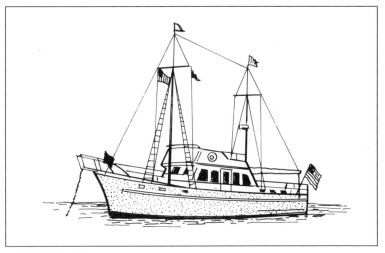

This documented two-masted vessel flies a Union Jack at the bow, a meal pennant on the port spreader, a club burgee on the mainmast, a private signal on the mizzen, a USPS ensign on the starboard spreader, and the yacht ensign on the stern.

days and holidays, and only at anchor, never when under way. (At a mooring or at the dock is acceptable, too.) It is flown at the bow, either on a jackstaff or secured vertically to the forestay. Be sure to fly it right side up, stars pointing up, in the "shed water" position.

Other Flags

T he Owner Absent flag is a rectangular blue flag displayed under the starboard spreader, at anchor or under way, whenever the owner is not on board. (If guests or family members are aboard without the owner, the guest flag, a blue rectangle with a white diagonal stripe, should fly instead.) While not frequently seen, these flags remain useful to signal the owner's friends that the vessel may be under charter or on a delivery trip.

The owner's meal flag, a white rectangular flag, flies at the starboard spreader at appropriate times on large yachts. A red pennant under the port spreader signifies crew mealtime.

The Night Hawk, a long blue pennant or windsock, flies in place of all other flags on sailboats at the masthead, after colors (at night). It allows the night watch to check wind direction easily.

A Homeward Bound pennant, rarely seen today, is a long, skinny (15:1) flag that was flown by fishing vessels and merchant ships on their homeward passage. It is horizontally divided into two halves, red and white, with a blue canton with stars.

A single code flag flying from the bow pulpit or from the backstay indicates that the boat is actively engaged in racing. It represents the class number of that boat, assigned to her for that race by the Race Committee.

Other commonly used single code flags are the red code flag B, used to initiate a protest in sailboat racing; the yellow code flag Q, to request customs clearance in foreign ports; and the tricolor T flag,

23

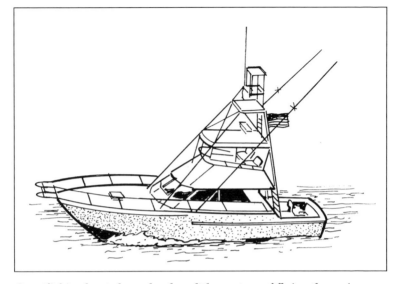

Sportfishing boats have developed the custom of flying the ensign from the tuna tower.

hoisted at the starboard spreader when launch service is requested.

Sportfishing boats fly special flags to signify their catch, and the yacht club officers fly special flags in place of their club burgee to denote their rank in the club. These are prescribed in the club's bylaws.

The red rectangular flag with the white diagonal stripe denotes "diver down" and is flown by boats actively attending a diver under water. While the official diver's flag is a "rigid replica" of code flag A, the red flag is generally recognized as the diving flag. It should not be flown by a boat going to and from the dive site.

While not actually a flag, the black anchoring ball should be displayed above the foredeck of larger vessels at anchor. At night it is replaced by the anchor light, a 360-degree white light over the foredeck or on the masthead.

The Courtesy Flag

T he courtesy flag is the national flag of the nation the yacht is visiting. It should be flown from the forward starboard spreader hoist as soon as customs are cleared and the yellow Q flag comes down. It should be flown both under way and at anchor or dockside, and should be about half the size of the national ensign. Mastless vessels may use the bow staff for the courtesy flag.

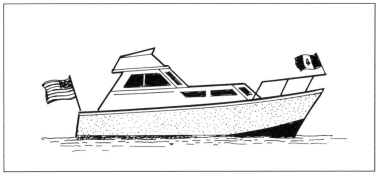

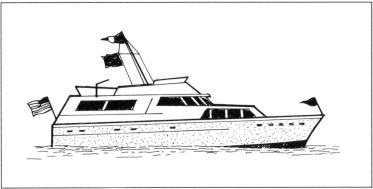

On a boat with no mast, the courtesy flag flies at the bow. If available, the starboard spreader hoist is the best location for the courtesy flag.

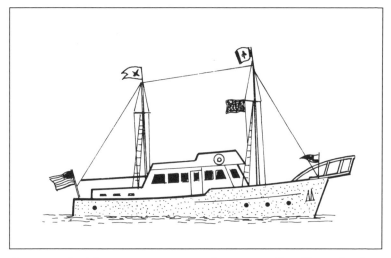

On a vessel with two or more masts, the courtesy flag flies under the forward starboard spreader.

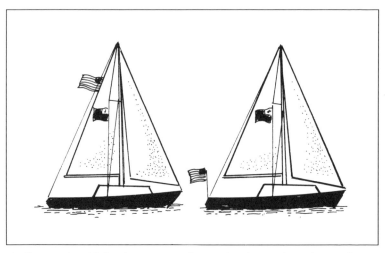

Sailboats should fly the courtesy flag under the starboard spreader, whether under sail or at anchor.

Dressing Ship

Most yachts use their set of code flags only to dress ship for holidays and special events. The International Code Flags are a time-honored and much under-utilized form of communication among vessels. The forty small, colorful flags comprise twenty-six rectangular letter flags, ten pennant-shaped numeral flags, three pennant-shaped flags called first, second, and third repeaters, and the "answering pennant." Their use is described in the *International Code*

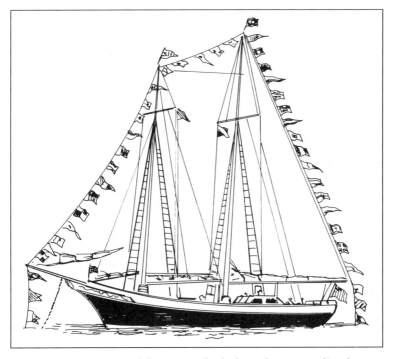

Dressing ship, the signal flags encircle the boat from waterline forward, to masthead, to waterline aft.

of Signals, H.O. Pub. No. 102, mentioned earlier, and they are still used in ship-to-ship communications.

For national holidays, special occasions, and launchings, yachts may "dress" while in port between 8 A.M. and sunset. All code flags (without flags such as burgees or the Union Jack) are strung together and raised to the masthead(s) and out to the boat's fore and aft extremities, whether it be the tip of the bowsprit or the overhanging boom. The line of flags should "encircle" the boat, from the waterline forward, aloft to the top of each mast, and down to the waterline aft; a flag or two should hang off the bow and off the stern, held secure by small weights.

The order of the flags is not important since they carry no more than a festive message, but they look best when they alternate two letter flags with one numeral pennant. A handy sequence is: AB2, UJ1, KE3, GH6, IV5, FL4, DM7, PO third repeater, RN first repeater, STO, CX9, WQ8, ZY second repeater.

The ensign, the burgees, and the Union Jack may be hoisted in their proper locations at the same time. A yacht should not get under way while "dressed" unless she is in a parade or on her maiden or final voyage.

CHAPTER THREE

HARBOR MANNERS

T here is a legend in the history of automobiles describing the first car accident. The first two cars in Ohio, the only two cars in Ohio, arrived at an intersection at the same time. Neither one wished to give way to the other. The drivers weren't use to it; they were used to being almost the only car in the state, and proceeding unimpeded. So, lacking the common sense that two horses might have shown at the same intersection, they collided.

Fortunately, boating is not quite as unregulated as those two cars in Ohio. We have the Rules of the Road, a marvelous, thoroughly tested body of rules that allows boats of many descriptions to navigate the same waters at the same time, in safety. It is just about impossible for two vessels to collide if each skipper knows and understands the Rules of the Road.

Though there is no substitute for a thorough reading of the Rules of the Road (see chapter 5 of *Chapman Piloting,* "Rules of the Road: Right-of-Way and Sound Signals"), a few of the most important rules bear repeating at every opportunity. These guidelines are from the Steering and Sailing Rules, which are almost identical for the U.S. Inland Rules and the International Rules.

Vigilance

T he first rule of the sea is constant vigilance. In practice, the person at the helm of a pleasure boat becomes the lookout, but the skipper or watch captain, or the person with the greatest experience, must keep a lookout, too. This is probably the greatest failing in pleasure boats: the person at the helm leaves the wheel for a soda, hoping the boat will stay on course; an inexperienced operator panics at the wheel and turns into another boat; the autopilot lulls the person at the helm into forgetting to look ahead as the boat plows steadily onward; or the sails prevent a clear view to leeward. It is easy to let vigilance slip, especially when few boats or hazards are around and the eyes on deck get complacent, or when everyone is concentrating so hard on some task at hand.

When visibility is less than perfect, every means available should be used to keep up vigilance. Listen for other boats, use the radar, and make systematic observations of anything that appears on the screen, and assign someone to do nothing but watch. In extremely low visibility, be sure to do everything you can to be seen by other boats: sound the horn in foggy conditions, use the correct navigation lights at night, and carry as big a radar reflector as you can. (Don't forget the old remedy of balled-up aluminum foil and empty soda cans wrapped up in a plastic garbage bag and hoisted aloft, or as high as possible, if you find yourself without a reflector in poor visibility.)

Don't rely on your instruments, no matter how sophisticated they might be. Boats with accurate loran sets can hit the navigational buoy they intended to round; two boats with operating radars can collide as they misjudge the other's speed or course. Keep a lookout at all times: constant vigilance.

A useful method for determining when the risk of a collision exists is the rule of constant bearings. Say you are at the helm of a small boat under power and see a big powerboat proceeding toward you on your starboard bow. You visually line up the powerboat with a lifeline stanchion or a fixture near the rail of your boat, say a cleat, without changing course. You watch the bearing, the line-up between the other boat and the cleat, as the powerboat gets closer. If the powerboat stays in line with the cleat as it approaches, then there is a danger of collision. The bearing has remained the same. The Rules of the Road then come into play, and your boat must give way, altering course or speed. This is a particularly useful trick to tell to neophytes at the helm because it helps them concentrate on the potential for collision, to maintain a constant watch on a boat in view, and to give useful information to the skipper on the risk of collision.

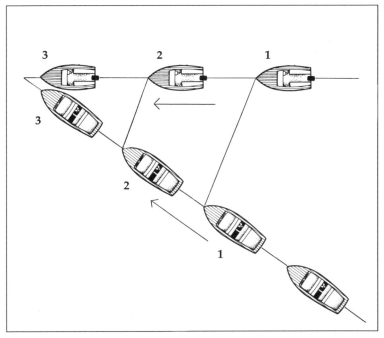

A risk of collision exists if the relative bearing between boats remains the same.

Keep an eye out on behalf of your neighbor on the water, too. If you see a boat dragging something over the side, such as a swimming ladder, a dock line, or a bathing suit, tell them; the people on board will probably be glad to hear about it before it is lost overboard. Point it out if you see a boat dragging her anchor, chafing her mooring lines, or rubbing against a piling. Point out hazards in the water, such as half-submerged logs, to boats following in your wake. Generally look out for the other guy's well-being at the dock and under way. Turn it around the other way: You would be happy to know if you were about to lose gear overboard, if your boat smelled of explosive gasoline fumes, if your tender broke loose or your lines nearly chafed through, before bad things actually happened.

Safe Speed

E very vessel must proceed at a safe speed at all times. As simple as this important rule is, it does not tell you what a safe speed might be. One boat's idle speed might be another boat's breakneck speed, and what was a safe speed yesterday is not necessarily safe today. Here is where the skipper's experience and judgment come into play. The Rules provide some guidelines for determining a safe speed in given conditions.

Visibility:
In heavy rain or fog, or at dusk or night, your boat's speed should be slow enough to allow you to see any boat ahead of you, and to allow you time to change course safely. Boat speed should also factor in any limits on visibility placed by the boat itself, for example a high bow obscuring the view forward, or a rain soaked windshield.

Traffic Density:

If the waters are crowded, you have to drop down from cruising speed. You may need to reduce speed just to figure out who has the right-of-way between you and every boat approaching you. A slow speed will give you and all the other skippers enough time to calculate what is going on. You may think you have it under control until the boat next to you surprises you with a quick change of course. If evasive action is necessary or if you are the "give-way" vessel (the "burdened" vessel in the old parlance) a change of course to avoid one vessel will put you in danger of collision with another.

Most harbors have a posted speed limit, marked by small buoys with "5 MPH" on them or with a big sign on land. Some busy stretches of water are designated as speed zones, comparable to a school zone on land. Florida waters in particular have many miles of speed zones limiting boat speed or designated as no wake zones. Tickets and fines can be issued. On one narrow stretch of the Intracoastal Waterway in the Carolinas where local children in small boats play near the channel, a stiff fine is due and payable at the time of the violation, which means that the harbormaster's boat comes alongside and waits for the cash, presently about eighty dollars. The speeder is hauled into the dock if no payment is forthcoming. This hard-nosed enforcement policy has evoked a lot of criticism, but boats move through the area at greatly reduced speeds.

Whether posted with speed limits or not, few harbors are able to enforce their speed limits as effectively as they should. State and local governments are always quick to cut monies for the harbor patrol from their budgets, and their many other duties often prevent harbormasters from lying in wait for speeders. It is too often left to the skipper's judgment (and willpower) as to how fast his or her boat should go, and when you have paid big bucks for a boat that can do fifty MPH, and no one is standing by to tell you otherwise, it gets tempting to just lean on the throttle and go. Therein lies one of the biggest hazards on the water, the boats that can't seem to slow down in congested areas. The Rules of the Road require a "safe speed," but don't say what it is, the harbormaster is too busy to give tickets to all the speeders, and most boats are designed to do many times the speed limit. What to do? It is up to the individual skipper to judge and maintain a safe speed, to consider the safety and comfort of all the boats nearby, and to set a good example to skippers with less experience and less judgment. Lives are lost and property damaged when judgment fails.

Maneuverability:

Your own vessel's maneuverability will help determine your speed. A big heavy vessel must proceed at a speed slow enough to allow for a quick stop or turn in spite of her way and momentum. Even more important, your boat's maneuverability is limited by how well the person at the helm can handle the vessel. If he or she doesn't realize that the stern is going to swing much wider than the bow in a tight turn, it's better that this be learned at a slow speed.

Consider the sea conditions in determining your speed. Choppy seas will make the boat pound unnecessarily, while a slower speed will allow most boats to ride easily over the same seas. Speed is one of the most important elements in storm tactics and in safe boat-handling in rough conditions. Control of the boat's speed in rough weather is one of the most difficult aspects of good seamanship, whether for sail- or powerboats, and whole books are written on the topic. And remember: For many smaller boats, rough conditions may be the product of a passing boat or two, not only a passing squall.

Navigational Hazards:

Keep in mind the depth of the water, and your draft. Obviously, it is better to run aground at half speed than at full speed. Most boats fitted with depth sounders have a readout at the helm to record how much water is under the keel: they are often fitted with alarms to warn of shallow water. But if you are going too fast the alarm will do you no good, as you won't have time to change course; you'll just hit bottom as the alarm sounds.

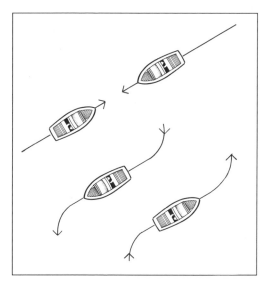

*Course changes
should be large
enough to be noticed
early.*

*Specific rights apply
to every vessel meet-
ing other vessels.*

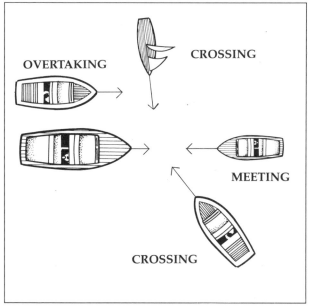

OVERTAKING

CROSSING

MEETING

CROSSING

No Wake

Y ou are responsible for any damage caused by your wake. Big rolling wakes are one of the most troublesome aspects of speed. Wakes are not mentioned in the Rules of the Road, but a safe speed at all times is an important part of the Rules, and wakes are a function of speed. Minding your wake by controlling your speed is of great importance to the safety of all vessels. Even a tug with barge can sustain damage when a big plea-sure-boat wake rolls in, sending the barge crashing into the tug.

You never know what damage your wake might be inflicting on other boats. Being rolled about by a wake is not merely annoying, though it is that, too. It can be dangerous to very small boats that can be quickly swamped, sending their occupants for an unexpected swim. It is almost as though every speeding boat leaves storm conditions for the boats behind her, kicking up waves usually reserved for a gale and sending them from shore to shore. A big wake can roll boats of any size into the pier or against their lines, causing damage to the lines, the boat, the pier, or even the people who may be fending off the pier. Particularly in otherwise calm waters, a wake can cause distress and discomfort. A quiet marina can turn into an instant maelstrom with all the boats pitching, masts tangling, and drinks flying when a thoughtless powerboat steams down the channel nearby, pulling too big a wake.

Whistle Signals

I n a crowded commercial harbor where tugs and ferry boats criss-cross the channel and oilers and tankers glide close by one anoth-er, the radio is often filled with cryptic communications on naviga-tional matters. "Pass you on one whistle, skipper" or "Coming up on your stern with two whistles." Whether these coded messages are exchanged on VHF channel 13 between bridges, or delivered by the horn blasts themselves, they refer to the sound signals.

Sound signals are required by the Rules of the Road for all powered vessels approaching within one-half mile of one another. Too few pleasure boats take the time to observe the simple signals properly; their value is underestimated. Like the use of flags on a yacht, proper use of signals marks the skipper as a courteous observer of the traditions of the sea, and as a knowledgeable communicator. Unlike flags, the use of signals can add a great deal to the safety of the vessel that uses them correctly, which is why they are prescribed in the Rules of the Road.

There are only five signals you need to know. The most important is the Danger Signal—five or more short blasts on the horn. It means "Stop your intentions!" or "Danger ahead!" It is sounded whenever one skipper considers another skipper's actions dangerous to either skipper's boat. If you hear five blasts on the horn, slow down immediately until you can determine what the perceived danger might be.

Three blasts on the horn means "My engines are in reverse." This might mean that the boat giving the signal is going backward, or it might mean she is stopping suddenly. Three blasts are given when a boat backs out of a slip, warning boats nearby of the maneuver.

One short blast on the horn means "I intend to leave you on my port side," or in the International Rules, "I am altering course to starboard," which is really the same thing if you think about it. Like two cars on a narrow roadway, boats customarily pass port side to port side whenever they meet head on, making the appropriate course change to starboard as they approach one another and sound one short blast. They communicate and agree on this simple maneuver when one boat sounds a short blast (either boat may initiate the exchange) and then the other boat answers with the same single short blast. If either skipper sees danger in this intended action, the danger signal of five blasts is sounded. Neither vessel should proceed until a new agreement is reached through further signals or through VHF radio channel 13 on one watt of power, or through channel 16.

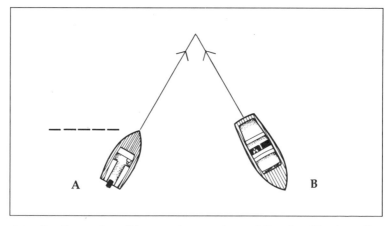

In a situation such as this, a mariner must sound five short blasts on the horn (represented by the dashes) to indicate danger: stop your intentions.

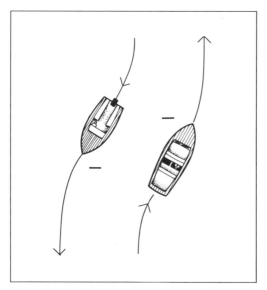

Both boats sound one blast and both alter course to starboard.

Two short blasts on the horn (in the Inland Rules) means, "I intend to leave you on my starboard side," which amounts to the same thing as the International Rules definition of "I am altering course to port." It should be answered by two short blasts from the approaching vessel, resulting in an orderly starboard side to starboard side meeting, or passing

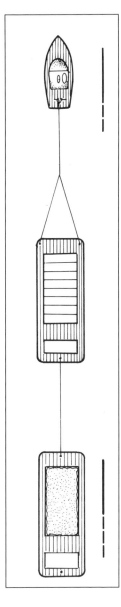

The vessel being towed sounds one long—three short blasts in reduced visibility immediately after the towing boat sounds its own signal.

a slower vessel on her port side.

One long blast should be sounded by a vessel entering a channel from a berth to alert other vessels in the channel of her action. A vessel entering a channel has no right-of-way over boats already in the channel, just as cars entering the highway must give way to the cars already proceeding along the highway.

Unfortunately for sailboats with their engines turned off, sound signals are not used between two approaching boats under sail. This omits a valuable means of communication from their repertoire. Of course, sail–

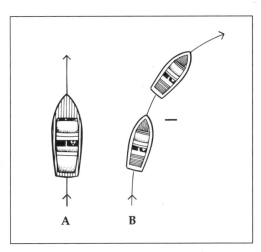

In the International Rules, course changes are signaled, but the signal is not returned by other vessels.

boats using their engines are considered powerboats and can make use of the signals above.

Note that these sound signals are to be used whenever vessels are clearly in sight of one another, at one-half mile apart and closing. They are not to be used in fog or at night, when the signals for reduced visibility are used.

The basic signal given in fog is one long blast about every two minutes when under way. A vessel restricted in her ability to maneuver, and that includes boats under sail, tugs pushing barges, vessels constrained by their draft, and vessels engaged in fishing, all sound the same signal: one long blast followed by two short blasts. Other signals indicate other types of vessels in poor visibility, for example, a vessel being towed (or the last barge in a string) should sound one long blast then three short blasts right after the towing vessel sounds her signal of one long and two short blasts. These and other signals are given in detail in chapter 5 of *Chapman Piloting*.

Where signals are concerned, the International Rules of the Road differ slightly from the Inland Rules. The International Rules require the one and two blast signals whenever a vessel plans to change course, as described above, but these signals need not be answered by other vessels, unless the approaching vessel will be taking a similar change of course, as happens quite often when two boats agree to make a port-to-port meeting.

Passing Techniques

W hen one boat overtakes another, there is a simple procedure that allows both boats to cause the least possible disruption to one another's progress and that makes the maneuver more comfortable for both boats. The procedure was developed and perfected in the Intracoastal Waterway, the 1,200-mile stretch of protected water that runs the length of the Eastern seaboard where hundreds of boats proceed at different speeds down the same channel. The passing procedure is needed because of the problem that arises when a faster boat, say a trawler proceeding at eight knots, wishes to pass a sailboat motoring along at six knots. The trawler pulls a big wake at eight knots, yet cannot slow down to reduce her wake and still maintain a passing speed. The passing maneuver takes a long while with only a two-knot speed differential, and the big wake rolls the sailboat the whole time. The sailboat skipper shakes his or her fist because the boat rolls mercilessly, and the trawler captain is furious because so much time is spent at the edge of the channel. It happens to each boat ten times in a day.

The slower boat can show good seamanship, as well as the utmost courtesy and graciousness, by initiating the procedure: The sailboat's skipper drops the boat's speed down to dead low or even idle just as

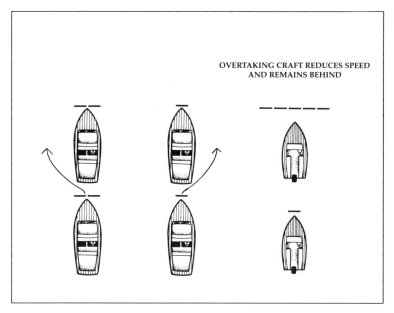

An orderly exchange of horn signals clarifies a passing maneuver.

the faster boat nears the stern. The overtaking boat will be able to drop her speed down to where there is no wake, yet maintain sufficient speed to pass quickly, say at five knots in our example. The whole maneuver takes only a minute, then both boats resume their cruising speeds, with their skippers in a much happier frame of mind. The time or momentum lost in throttling back briefly is easily rewarded by the quickness of the whole passing maneuver. The overtaken boat is not rolled around, and the overtaking boat is soon back in center channel at normal speed.

Right-of-Way

A boat approaching on your starboard side has right-of-way, and you must alter course to go astern or adjust your speed to get out of her way. The other boat, the "stand-on" vessel (also called the "privileged" vessel), should maintain course and speed while you maneuver around her. (Note the courtesy mentioned earlier in which both boats reduce their speed to expedite a passing maneuver.)

All vessels, under sail or power, give the right-of-way to fishing vessels when they are actively engaged in fishing and to any vessel with limited maneuverability, including very large vessels, tugs with barges, even pleasure boats too large to make a quick course change.

Right-of-Way for Sailboats

Sailboats have the right-of-way over boats under power that are not engaged in fishing and not limited in their maneuverability. This needs some clarification, because sailboat skippers think that when under sail they have the right-of-way over all other vessels. It just isn't so.

Sailboats with their engines on are considered powerboats in the Rules. It isn't enough that the sails are up and drawing, that the boat is heeling nicely or getting most of her speed from the sails. If the engine is on, the sailboat is considered a powerboat and loses all rights as a sailboat. She must steer clear of other sailboats without their engines on, and is subject to the Rules of the Road like any other powerboat.

If a sailboat is overtaking a boat under power, even if she is under sail alone, she must give right-of-way to the powerboat. This happens frequently in the cases of fast catamarans and sailboards.

If the boat under power is less maneuverable or is constrained by her draft, then the boat under sail must keep clear. This should prevent the little twenty-four-foot sailboat from sailing across the bow of a tugboat, or even in front of a large pleasure boat in the channel. All too often, the small-sailboat skippers give themselves the right to interfere with the larger boat's passage when in fact the larger, less maneuverable vessel should be allowed to proceed under the Rules.

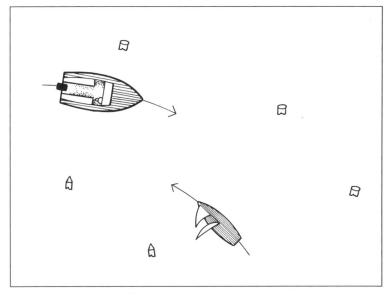

The boat under sail must keep clear of a boat confined to the channel.

More Rules for Sailboats

Between sailboats under sail, there are special rules to prevent collisions. They are arbitrary and should be memorized by every sailboat skipper and anyone else who may take the helm.

The vessel on the starboard tack, that is, with the wind crossing her starboard side first (with the starboard side "up" if the boat is heeling), has right-of-way over the boat on the port tack.

When both boats are on the same tack, the boat to leeward (the boat that gets the wind second) has the right-of-way.

When you are on the port tack and are approaching another sailboat, but you cannot tell what tack she is on, you must assume she is on the starboard tack and that she has right-of-way.

Finally, a whole book of rules for sailboats during a race is available from the U.S. Yacht Racing Union in Newport, Rhode Island. Racing sailboats need to carry a copy of these rules on board.

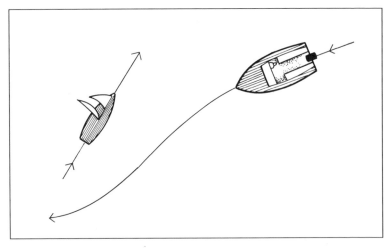

The powerboat alters course to avoid a boat under sail.

Sailboat skippers have to realize that nonsailors have no idea why sailboats have to zigzag so much, or why their course changes so frequently. To nonsailors, sailboats seem like the rudest boats on the water because they sail slowly down the center of the channel, capriciously change course 90 degrees, and vary their course this way and that as though avoiding logs. When a sailboat is the stand-on vessel, which she frequently is, she is under obligation to maintain her course and speed, so other vessels can plan their maneuvers around her. Skippers of racing sailboats frequently annoy other skippers with their self-absorbed maneuvering: You go out of your way to avoid the sailboat, which then changes course to get in the way again. And then the skipper rudely shakes a fist at you. Those skippers must realize that they are subject to the Rules of the Road during the race, even if it is not to their tactical advantage to be the burdened vessel.

The Gracious Gesture

In very congested waters, where pleasure boats of all descriptions are changing course this way and that to avoid one another, some understanding between boats beyond the basic navigation rules becomes essential. Radio communication may not work to clarify all the maneuvering necessary, whistle signals would fill the air with blasts from every direction, and all vessels, even a vessel with the right-of-way, would have to slow down and consider all the turmoil.

While it is so important to know the Rules of the Road yourself, and to handle your boat accordingly, it is equally important to know that the skipper on the boat approaching you knows the rules, too. How do you know this? You observe the other boat carefully. You watch her course, check that the person at the wheel or tiller sees you coming, adjusts the boat's course early if appropriate, or maintains his or her course while observing your course carefully. Knowledge and constant vigilance are required.

There is a courtesy on the water not prescribed in the Rules of the Road, but of great use to nonprofessional mariners. It is a means of communication not generally available to large vessels, but it accounts for much of the safe maneuvering among small (under forty feet) pleasure boats. This is the gracious gesture of "After you, captain." It may be a friendly wave across the water at an approaching vessel, and the simple acknowledgement that the other person sees you coming, or it may be a timely change of course to avoid a developing right-of-way situation. When a big powerboat motors slowly down the channel, the small-sailboat skipper might gesture with an arm to indicate that the powerboat, which might well be the give-way vessel, should proceed on course while the sailboat makes a small course-change. It happens all the time, in a manner similar to two people passing through a doorway at the same time. And so a better understanding develops between boats, and a better day—not to mention a safer day—on the water is had by all concerned

The Courtesies of Anchoring

W hen you set an anchor in the modern boating world, you have instant neighbors, often quite close by. In addition to securing a big enough anchor to an appropriate rode, giving it enough scope to dig into the bottom at an effective angle, and choosing a clear stretch of water with sufficient swinging radius (all of which is covered in detail in *Chapman Piloting*'s "Anchoring" chapter), you must consider your new neighbors. They will be carefully considering you. In many crowded anchorages, the hazard in the night is as likely to be your neighbor's boat as storm winds, high tide, low tide, or a change in the weather. It may also be a neighbor who shouts to waken you and tell you that you are dragging, which is much better than waking to the rudder grounding on a lee shore.

If every skipper practiced the rudiments of an effective anchor set, there would be less occasion for the exercise of good manners at anchor. Unlike a car, which stays when you put it in park, a boat will slither around on even a well-set anchor, and even the largest anchor and the most far-traveled skipper may drag from time to time. Knowledge, seamanship, and good gear should keep most boats out of trouble most of the time, but good manners may be needed when these are not enough to keep boats from "mixing it up" with one another late at night.

The dragging anchor must be hauled up and reset. If your boat is backing out of control into other boats, admit it at once. Don't argue; don't wait for the anchor to dig in. You'll save yourself time and trouble. Haul up the anchor and reset it promptly in another location and/or anchor with heavier gear.

The boat that anchors second must haul up and reset her anchor should she interfere with a boat that anchored earlier. The boat that anchored first has the right to stay where she is, assuming her own anchor has not dragged. Often the boat that put her anchor down first assumes that she need not reset it, even when she drags into another boat. That is when you hear the screaming match: "You were there, I was here." "No, you were there, I was here." Note that the first rule is that the dragging anchor must be hauled and reset.

Don't anchor among moored boats. Boats that are moored may be "at home" and unattended, or they may be paying good money to the owner of the mooring or the harbormaster to lie on that mooring in safety. In either case, they will have different swinging radii from that of anchored boats, and the anchored boat must move if there is trouble.

Don't anchor among empty moorings either. Their owners will probably return, and they have a right to ask for their full swinging room. The anchored boat has to move again.

Don't anchor close by another boat if you can comfortably anchor further away.

Use an anchor light or a 360-degree white masthead light to show your presence to other boats under way. This is part of the Rules of the Road and is a very good practice too often forgotten. A bow light, masthead tricolor, or masthead strobe will not do as an anchor light: They signify you are under way, or in distress. If you feel you need additional lights at night for safety, leave the cabin lights or the spreader lights on; they have no legal significance or meaning and effectively show your presence to other boats.

Keep the noise down on your boat: Loud music, partying, generators, children, dogs, and snapping halyards can be annoying to people who have gone to extra trouble to anchor just to get away from the hubbub of shore life.

Be mindful of local town ordinances that apply to anchored boats. Though not always adequately posted or charted, restrictions on the length of time you may remain at anchor, whether you may live aboard, whether two or more boats may raft up, or whether overboard sewage discharge is permitted, may affect your visit. These restrictions have sprung up as a result of abuses over the years and can seem rather strident; they may or may not be enforced. Keep in mind also that you may be asked to pay a fee to marinas for services ashore which might be free to paying dockside customers, such as dinghy tie-up, garbage disposal, fresh water, car parking, and, of course, showers. Marinas and other waterfront establishments may have tremendous costs associated with these services, though they may seem minor to you, and it is only fair to pay them a small fee for the use of their facilities.

Rafting-up

The rafting of friendly yachts, one next to the other, is one of the joys of convivial cruising, and in clement weather, can increase the capacity of a small harbor, as well as the deck space available for a party. The procedure for rafting-up is about the same as making an approach to a dock, except that the dock is swinging back and forth, and may have a swaying mast which can tangle dangerously with other masts at the spreaders. The use of spring lines becomes especially important.

Except in harbors like Cuttyhunk, off the coast of Massachusetts, where boats are assigned three to a mooring (each paying its own fee) by the harbormaster, rafting is usually by mutual agreement between skippers, or by a mothership tending to the needs of a smaller or racing vessel. Boats may raft on a mooring or on the largest boat's anchor, but if more than one anchor is needed, consider making another raft. When more than one anchor is used, they may tangle or drastically alter the strains on all the lines as the boats turn.

Rafting is safe only if all vessels in the raft are attended at all times: A capable person must be aboard each boat in case the anchor begins to drag and the raft must break up promptly. Every boat should be prepared to depart the raft and take care of herself should the weather change. If a change is expected, the raft should break up while it is still light, before darkness makes anchoring more difficult.

Even rafted among friends, crew should ask permission to step aboard, or to cross the deck to another boat, before doing so for the first time. Privacy is harder to maintain in a large raft, and so it is all the more precious: Cross the foredeck rather than walking through the cockpit, tread lightly as you cross the deck to minimize the noise and reduce the rolling of the boat.

CHAPTER FOUR

DOCKSIDE MANNERS

Approaching the Dock

A ny landing that causes no damage is a successful landing. Beyond that there are a few courtesies, mentioned below, that will make a happier landing. Chief among them is that you must be sure your boat is welcome where you choose to tie up.

Reservations

A friendly hail across the water should secure a dock for smaller vessels, but radio contact via VHF radio works best in large harbors and for larger yachts. Many busy ports are booked up months in advance. These marinas should be phoned by landline as soon as you know when you plan to be there. A good source of marina phone numbers is the *Waterway Guide*, an annual guide published by Communication Channels. This publication also gives the VHF channel normally monitored by a particular marina, usually 16, 68, or 09.

Whether you have reservations or not, contact the marina only when you are within clear radio range. Don't clog the airwaves by trying to raise a marina which is still beyond range. In fact, many busy marinas prefer that you wait until you are within visual range so they can direct you to the appropriate pier right away. The marina should be able to tell you what side to place your fenders and docklines on, in preparation for docking. You should be able to tell them your departure date, fuel needs, water and electrical service, and repair needs.

Dockage rates often cannot be discussed over the airwaves. They may change from week to week, season to season.

Keep in mind that every marina, even the most decrepit one, is sitting on prime waterfront real estate, and that there are probably weekly pressures to build condos under the travellift. The people who own the marina could make a lot more money by selling out to developers. Operating a profitable marina is difficult at best; give the owners their due.

Private Docks
A small private dock in Newport has a sign reading, "Any boat left on this dock will be taken away and sunk at owner's expense." Not all private docks post such a sign, but you should steer as clear of private docks as if they did.

Docking
Making a good landing is not so much a matter of courtesy as a function of knowledge and forethought. Tidal current, wind, engine configuration, talent on the foredeck, and talent on the pier are factors almost as important as the handling at the helm, and must be carefully considered by the skipper. Good seamanship is shown by the skipper's careful coaching of everyone on the boat before the docking maneuver begins. Even the skipper of a small boat should inform the crew as to which slip they intend to enter, or what side of the boat will be at the dock. All fenders should be in place, at a height even with the dock, and evenly placed along the widest section of the hull. Docklines should be led clear of lifelines and staunchions, coiled neatly, then laid on the deck or held by a crewmember ready to throw them ashore. Fenderboards should be placed, if necessary, after all lines have been snugged up, so that the boat will rest stationary alongside the piling.

Handling a Line

C rew members should understand where each line on the boat is intended to go on the dock. Is this a forward spring or a stern spring? They will probably have occasion to tell someone taking the line which way it is supposed to go. If they don't know, they can ask the skipper. If the skipper doesn't know, consult the chapter on "Power Cruiser Seamanship" in *Chapman Piloting*. Crew members can tell the dock attendant not to snub up too quickly (the cause of many a botched landing), to put the eye splice around a certain piling, or to cleat it fast to ease the boat alongside. It is the skipper's job to see that this is all understood and carried out without much yelling. A good skipper never blames the crew or the current for a botched land-

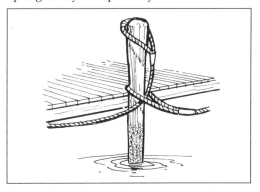

One eye can be passed through another on a piling so that either can be removed easily.

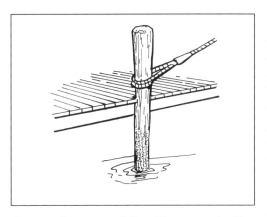

An extra loop around the piling prevents slippage up or down.

ing; it is the skipper's failure to communicate the vessel's needs to the crew or a miscalculation of the conditions that will botch things up. The more discussion that goes on before docking, the better the chances for a quiet and orderly maneuver.

Anyone handling a dockline should learn how to throw it properly, extending its full length and reaching its destination. Learn to coil a line quickly, in big, even coils, in case it should fail to reach the dock on the first throw. Separate the line roughly in half, holding half of the coil in each hand. Throw the first half high across the dock, in a big sweeping gesture, almost like bowling in the air, and let the remaining coils follow. Coil quickly but very carefully if it falls short; more throws are spoiled by fouled line than by late timing. And do the dock attendant a favor; don't throw the wet, heavy line in his or her face. No one would be able to see it coming, much less catch it, while shielding the face for self-protection. Aim the line to land on the dock, at the feet of a grateful attendant.

Fenders

Fenders, too frequently called bumpers, are simple and useful devices, yet they are so often sloppily used that they have become a mark of poor nautical etiquette all by themselves. The rule for fenders is: A boat under way should never be seen with its fenders over the side. When she is dockside, naturally she will use all fenders necessary. As soon as she is away from the dock, a yacht's fenders should be pulled up as promptly as is humanly possible, so that at no time could a shoreside onlooker see a boat under way with fenders adangle.

If you should see a boat that has failed to ship the fenders, and they are dangling and banging over the side in the bow wave, point it out to the skipper politely. If the skipper responds that the boat will soon be docking, or has just come from the dock, ask the skipper if he (or her husband) leaves his fly undone on the way to or from the bathroom. The affront to good manners is about equal.

Pets Aboard

T ake your dogs and cats, monkeys and birds aboard with you wherever you go. Animals are usually well-liked on the water and they make good cruising companions. Unfortunately, too many dogs go unchaperoned, making a mess on the pier or up on the yacht-club lawn, or yapping at dawn. Many marinas have posted rules or have prohibited pets entirely; it is easy to understand why if you have ever met a growling Chesapeake Bay retriever on the dock beside your cockpit. It shouldn't take a book on boating etiquette to tell people to curb their dog when ashore, leash it if it is fierce, and keep it from trespassing on other boats.

Noise

I t doesn't take a book on nautical etiquette to tell anyone that excessive noise is offensive. On the water it is a particular nuisance because sound travels great distances, offending the ears of many. Muscle boats, sounding like a jet plane right overhead, are big offenders when it comes to noise. Like motorcycles a decade ago, these boats despise mufflers, and they are responsible for their own bad reputations. Some townships have attempted to regulate the noise level on their waters, in addition to regulating speeds, although noise regulations are difficult to enforce.

Use of electrical generators can be annoying to neighbors late at night or early in the morning. Particularly at quiet anchorages, generators generate complaints.

Sailboats can be big offenders in the noise department, too. A very slight breeze can set halyards to tapping on the mast in the most irritating rhythm. No amount of tightening will cancel this rat-a-tat; the lines must be pulled away from the mast, either by securing them to the bow pulpit or lifelines, or by the use of gilguys, light line used to tie halyards out to the shrouds and away from the mast. Jon Wilson of *WoodenBoat* magazine has pointed out that a slapping halyard is just as offensive when it slaps on a wooden mast as on an aluminum mast, and that it may remove varnish, too. The Concordia Yard boatyard replaces the short gilguys on the Concordia yawls in their care every year, so that they will always be in place, ready for use, and to keep the yawls tidy.

Gilguys should tie off the halyards whether there is a breeze to make the halyards slap or not. It may be long after the owners have gone home that the breeze builds enough to set the halyards slapping, and that's when the boat in the next slip will start complaining about the noise. A modern equivalent to the noisy halyards is the noisy furling slot appearing in new rigs. It will howl like an empty soda bottle when you blow on it, yielding an unearthly low whistle. Ask your sailmaker for a stopper at the masthead if this noise emanates from your boat.

Noise in the form of loud music is as offensive in crowded harbors as it is from across the street, perhaps moreso because sound carries so well across the water. It is even worse in uncrowded harbors. Treat your maritime neighbors as you treat your neighbors ashore, or perhaps better than that.

Keep in mind that, because sound travels so well across the water, normal conversations carry much further than you may expect. This can be embarrassing when the subject of your conversation raises his or her head out of the companionway wearing a scowl.

CHAPTER FIVE

RADIO MANNERS

Misuse of the VHF radio is a real problem on busy waterways, where frequencies with specified uses are overcrowded with idle chatter between boats. The FCC has strict regulations for the use of VHF radios, but these regulations (given in *Chapman Piloting*, chapter 22, "Electronic Equipment: Communication") are not sufficient by themselves to keep the airways clear, and too many skippers seem unaware of the regulations anyway. Skippers must know the regulations, and have the courtesy to observe the intent of the regulations as well, particularly these:

1. Use Channel 16 for distress and hailing only.
2. Keep conversations as short as possible.
3. Use minimum power (one watt) whenever possible.
4. Listen before transmitting so you don't "step on" other calls.

Keep in mind the assigned purpose of the different VHF channels. Channel 16 is the most important one: It is the distress, safety, and call frequency. It is also the most abused channel. It should be monitored by all vessels whenever the radio is turned on but not actively in use. Transmissions should be brief in the extreme. *"Moonfleet, Moonfleet, Moonfleet.* This is the yacht *Saphaedra,* WJZ 1234. Come in please. Over."

"Saphaedra, this is the yacht *Moonfleet,* WYX 3212; switch and answer channel 72, channel 72."

The reply: "Switching to channel 72."

End of transmission on channel 16. If no reply is heard, wait two minutes before hailing again. If there is still no reply after three tries, hold off for fifteen minutes: Your party is not listening or is not within range. ("Over" may be omitted when the reception is good.)

Channel 6 is for the intership safety communications, with the emphasis on safety. Along with channel 16, all radios are required to have channel 6 (also given as 06).

Noncommercial craft, that is pleasure boats, have five assigned intership channels: 68 (the most popular), 69, 71, 72, and 78. To select a working channel, determine which of these is free of traffic before raising another vessel on channel 16, then switch to that channel as soon as contact is made.

Channel 70 used to be a common working channel but has been designated as a distress and safety calling channel for digital selective calling only. This will be a new high-tech transmission (not yet on line) that will broadcast special safety announcements.

Noncommercial boats should use channel 9 (or 09) to communicate with commercial vessels and with commercial shore facilities such as marinas and yacht clubs.

Channel 13 is for navigational matters between ships (large vessels must monitor channel 13 in addition to channel 16) in constricted waters, and an approaching barge can often be raised on channel 13. Army-operated locks and drawbridges usually monitor channel 13, too. It should always be used with only one watt of power.

The Coast Guard delivers safety messages on channel 22(A), which is also used by pleasure boats to converse with the Coast Guard, although it is basically reserved for the U. S. government.

Channels 25, 26, 27, 28, and 84 are the Marine Operator channels used to patch VHF radio calls into the local landlines, i.e., for ordinary phone calls home. On a Saturday evening in the boating season, these channels are nearly impossible to use because of the long waiting lists of callers, and the interminable listening you have to do while you wait your turn to make a call. You can wait for an hour by the radio to make your call and find out that nobody is home at the number you are trying to reach. Your calls are not private and cannot be made at a specific time due to the traffic. Cellular phones are a better alternative for the skipper who frequently needs landline service.

Skippers who want to contact another boat can plan ahead by pre-arranging a VHF channel to monitor at a certain time of day, or a certain time during every hour (such as twenty minutes after every hour). Most new radios can monitor two or more channels at once, so skippers can monitor a predetermined channel and channel 16 at the same time. This plan can free up channel 16 for other uses.

When you use your VHF radio (other than for calls through the Marine Operator—landline telephone calls) imagine that a small boat far away is in distress, sinking, or with someone overboard, and is trying desperately to contact someone on channel 16. Her batteries are low and her signal is weak. The distress call needs to get through, even more than your call to reserve a slip at the marina. Listen for that call before you key the mike. Think of that distress call trying to get through during your conversation about the size of bluefish, and keep your conversation short, even on a working frequency.

Think of that distress call when you blast away at full twenty-five-watt power to another boat close by, sending your signal much further than it needs to go and interfering with other calls. If you have ever made a distress call, or heard a distress call transmitted over the air, it is easier to remember the courtesies mentioned above, and the reasons for them. They are all directly related to safety on the water.

CHAPTER SIX

MANNERS ON THE RACECOURSE

R acing brings out many of the best and most knowledgeable sailors all at once in an organized group. The best boat handling, the best boats, the sharpest crews, and the most experienced skippers convene in high concentration on a racecourse. They know the racing rules like sea lawyers, can handle adverse weather and sea conditions like veterans of ocean wars, and know the bearing and "distance off" of every boat in the fleet. Yet some evil mood often accompanies racing fleets, causing fine sailors to forget their own kindly natures, their good manners, and something more important as well: The skipper at the helm of a racing sailboat sometimes seems to forget the Rules of the Road, which apply to them just as much as they do to other boats of varying types enjoying the water.

Good Manners for Race Participants

I n addition to the bonds of good fellowship set by the other competitors, and the level of sportsmanship established by the sponsoring club or committee, racing skippers should be bound by their knowledge of the Rules of the Road. This would seem fairly obvious, but it is too often forgotten in the heat of close competition. Racing sailboats have no special rights of way; they are not mentioned in the Rules of the Road, except as sailboats. They rarely qualify as "least maneuverable vessel" or as "restricted in her ability to maneuver." They are usually highly maneuverable; their skippers just don't want to give an inch. Somehow the skippers see only the competitors in their own fleet; other boats are almost invisible. They often seem surprised by the close proximity of a nonracing boat and are not prepared to change course. They certainly won't alter speed to avoid a confrontation, but will keep up their racing trim. In the highest levels of racing, where the skippers should know the Rules well, manners may be just as bad as those in the junior racing program, or perhaps much worse.

The Rules say nothing about a boat stealing wind from the sails of another boat; so why is it that a cruising boat passing within five boat-lengths of a racing boat is subjected to contemptuous shouts of rage as if he had stolen the trophy? The Rules do not permit a sailboat to cross slowly in front of a tug and barge coming down the channel; yet many tugboat captains in Long Island Sound have premature gray hair from leaning on the throttle in hard reverse to avoid a tiny self-righteous sailboat. The Rules do not suggest that the give-way vessel can become the stand-on vessel by dint of rude and offensive exclamations designed to intimidate the privileged vessel into altering course immediately. The racing boat, like every other boat, must consider her right-of-way as outlined in the Rules of the Road and then act accordingly. Even if the racing boat does have the right-of-way, she cannot alter course (e.g., tack or jibe, or bear off sharply) while another vessel is maneuvering around her. As well as studying the Racing Rules (to see, for example, who has a "mast abeam" or an overlap), racing skippers should know the Rules of the Road cold.

And if nonracing boats should have the courtesy and good manners to stay out of a racing boat's wind, and throw no wake to shake the sails, and if tugs and tows should cross clear ahead, the racing sailboat must consider herself lucky, although there will be no good excuse to lose the race.

Good Manners for Spectators

R acing requires tremendous concentration by the participants, and precise courses are set not to the compass, but to the shifting wind direction. In a breeze the boats will be on a fine edge balancing crew weight with sail area, and a gap in the concentration of the person at the helm can spill the occupants out of the boat in a second. The skipper and crew on the rail will be all too aware of their fine balance, and perhaps nervous about it. They may react badly when their balance is threatened. The smaller the boat, the greater the chance for a swim, and the more enraged the skipper will be if his or her balance is disturbed by the presence of another boat. For the sailor who has never raced a boat, it can be difficult to understand the seemingly capricious behavior of a serious racer; it behooves the nonracing boat to courteously avoid the racing boats altogether.

If you see a bunch of similar sailboats all pointing in the same direction, you may assume that they are engaged in a race, and that they would prefer that a nonracing boat stay clear of the fleet as a whole. If it is possible to alter course or speed to circumnavigate the fleet, then do so before any conflicts of course cause the racers to lose their concentration, and before any right-of-way situation arises. Take the stern of the last boat in the fleet. Even the straggler will be irate if you cross the bow and throw a wake.

By calculating which buoy or marker the fleet may be aiming for, you may be able to determine the turning mark of the racecourse, and avoid the fleet as a whole again after they change course and head the other way. Race courses are usually triangular, like the America's Cup

Course or the Olympic Course, with all marks of the course left to port, but they may be any shape the Race Committee signals to the fleet at the start. It may be nearly impossible to determine the progress of the fleet around the course, or even what mark they are headed for. Watch the first boat in the fleet to see the new direction of the course.

A fleet of large sailboats may be so spread out that each competitor looks like a lone cruising boat out for a sail. If the sails are carefully trimmed, and look like spider webs of high-tech ribbon, and if the crew is perched on the rail as though on the bleachers, then the boat may be part of a long-distance race. If it is calm, a boat in the thick of a race may look like a baking beach party, with sails flapping like laundry out to dry, going nowhere with the crew asleep on the foredeck. That crew may be just as mad when a wake rocks the boat and shakes what little wind there is out of the sails, and kills hard-won momentum.

Outside busy yacht harbors such as Annapolis, Marblehead, or San Francisco, there may be many, many fleets of gnatlike sailboats darting every which way. You will have to cut across one fleet or another in order to get anywhere at all. You must run the gauntlet of shouting racers as quickly as possible, observing the right-of-way rules and running no boats down. Wait a minute at idle speed to let the fleet pass if you have time; you may learn something about racing by observing the difference in sail trim or crew concentration on the first boat in comparison to the last boat. As in any congested harbor, every boat has to accommodate the other boats using the same waters by reducing speed, altering course, and sometimes signaling graciously for another boat to pass on her way across their course.

CHAPTER SEVEN

GUESTS ABOARD

A guest's work is never done.

Visiting at a friend's summer house for the weekend, you might expect to sleep late in the morning, enjoy a leisurely breakfast on the porch with the newspaper and the puppy, venture out to go antiquing or to pick apples for a pie, perhaps take a dip in the pool, drinks and a video after dinner. No work, no cleaning, no tidying up. Minimal exertion, maximal leisure.

A guest's function on a boat is usually as crew, and crew is expected to be active and keep busy. There is always more to do on a boat; and about the only chance you get to sit around and be idle is when you take the time to say "let's just sit for a minute" to watch the sunset, or to scrutinize another boat's anchoring detail nearby. Otherwise, all crew can expect to be on the go almost all of the time.

Even before the boat leaves dock, there are chores to do. If you are on a big powerboat, the windows on the bridge may need a freshwater rinse, the case of wine may need to be brought aboard and stowed, and the shore power cord may need to be coiled and stowed, all before the voyage begins. On a little sailboat going out for the weekend, the ice needs to come aboard at the last minute and the food stowed above it, and the duffles need to be jammed into the foot of the bunk. None of this kind of work requires great seafaring experience, so neophytes need not be idle; lots of chores that the skipper can and should delegate to the weekend guest always crop up. Of course if you are visiting Malcolm Forbes on the 130-foot *Highlander*, the uniformed crew serve hors d'oeuvres, and polish the brightwork for your inspection.

A good crew makes the skipper look smart, though the truth may be otherwise. They know where to stow their own gear (with a little hint) and where much of the ship's gear should be. When called upon to handle a piece of equipment, they know the general routine from stowing the docklines to operating the loran. They can make a line fast to a cleat without making one hundred turns to bury the cleat. They can show a less experienced crew member how to use the winch handle and how to put it back after every use.

Crew who have been on the boat before and are returning for more are the best crew to have, whether you are racing in the top levels or cruising across the bay. Perhaps they can recall glorious moments of past voyages, and therefore understand the boat's idiosyncrasies and how to deal with them. They know where the Phillips-head screwdriver is and how the icebox works; they might know the skipper's idiosyncrasies, too. Crew members such as these are a boat's greatest asset. They make a boat safer than the best safety equipment, faster than the latest new sail, and easier to handle than all the short-handed cruising gear put together. If and when you find a crew who enjoy the boat and the voyages you take together, bind them to you with bonds of love, money, or the promise of adventure; whatever works to guarantee their return. As good care as the skipper takes of the engine, the sails, the topsides, or the brightwork, he or she should take even better care of the regular guests.

Inexperienced crew can be almost as helpful as the expert, sometimes more helpful if their enthusiasm results in a willing hand. Skippers can become jaded about some of the simple pleasures of being on a boat, like the sounds of the boat, the change of light across the water, the novelty of the loran, or the power of the canvas. New crew help old crew to see again some of the mystery and excitement of boats; the skipper might for a moment forget the leaky sump tank and the prop wobble. It doesn't matter if the skipper didn't order the new sail or the latest electronic device, the guests are thrilled by how the boat throws a wave aside. It may help the skipper to see that something has gotten unnecessarily complicated, like using all the interfaced electronic devices to find the home mooring on a clear day.

Neophyte crew have to observe carefully how the experienced crew handle the boat, then ask questions about everything they don't understand. Much of basic boating, sail or power, is just common sense. On a well-run boat, there is a good reason for every esoteric device and procedure, though it may not be apparent. When the time seems right, ask why. If the skipper seems too busy to bother with too many questions of "What is that?", ask anyone else on board who seems knowledgeable. If you find yourself in the troubling situation of being the most experienced crew member and still not knowing what to do, ask the skipper directly, and hope for a good answer.

Guests can spend time practicing things which may come in handy later on. Try tying bowlines and rolling hitches in spare time. Figure-eight knots are very nautical and easy to tie and untie. Practice using your judgment of the right-of-way situations as they develop between other boats, and see how the skipper is judging his or her own boat's maneuverability and speed.

"All aboard? Let's go."
"Ready on the bow line? Fend off."
"All fenders on deck? Bring them aft."
"Got the docklines aboard? Coil them up."
"Got them coiled and ready to hang up? Stow them below."

67

"Got them stowed? Stow the fenders."
"Are they dirty? Clean them off."
"Got them clean? Take the docklines out again and put the fenders
    in first."
Endless.

Cooking

G uests may be asked to help prepare food in the galley, and no
one needs to shirk this duty, even if they categorically refuse to
enter a kitchen when ashore. It is quite a different job on a boat. (Dish-
washing remains about the same as its shoreside equivalent, or worse,
without the dishwasher, without the running hot water, practically
without any water.) Cooking aboard is always a creative endeavor,
challenging available foods to go together, preparing favorite dishes
without the regular ingredients, and preparing greater quantities of
everything.

The quantity of the food prepared is always more important than
the complexity, and it may be more important than the quality. Hungry crew will only complain about the cooking if there is not enough
food; they'll rarely complain otherwise. Happily, a decent cook gets a
disproportionate share of praise and affection, usually deserved and
always appreciated.

If the menus are kept simple, cooking can easily be done by any
willing guest. The cook can often collar other hapless crew to peel
potatoes, set the table, or slice the bread, and the work gets spread
around as needed. On a longer voyage, assigned cooking chores
spread the work load more equitably; however, someone must be
given full responsibility for the galley and the orderly distribution of
its contents.

Cleaning

C leaning jobs may be pleasanter on board a boat because the space to clean is always smaller than its landside equivalent. However, boats get dirtier than you might imagine even on short voyages. Cleaning chores need to be assigned or else they won't get done; no one ever volunteers to clean the head. Daily chores are mentioned in pages 87–89, in the section on the ship's daily routine. They need not fall to the guest all the time, though it may seem that way to the guest. At the end of a passage, guests should always help with the end-of-trip cleanup, which includes a wipe down of all surfaces below deck, particularly the head and galley, and a thorough sweeping up of the whole boat. Guests should not shirk this duty or slip away with this simple job undone.

The Skipper's Responsibility to Guests

I f the guests have to work hard to earn their keep on board, the skipper has an even greater responsibility to each guest. It falls to the skipper to make sure that every guest has a minimum of knowledge about safe procedures on board and actions and equipment to use in any kind of emergency. Guests may not know to ask for simple instruction on where the flares are stowed, where the fire extinguisher lies, or where their own life preserver is stowed. The skipper has to point out the safety equipment with care and sufficient emphasis that the guests will consider the possibilities of danger and remember where the equipment is stowed should it be needed in a hurry. The skipper is the one who stows the equipment and checks its operation, but it may be the guest who gets it out and uses it.

The skipper must also see that no hazards considered routine to experienced crew take a green sailor by surprise. Gear such as jibing booms, gimballed stoves with hot food, or luffing sails, can be deadly if their power or danger is not anticipated; lesser gear, such as cabinets that suddenly swing open, fishhooks near at hand, hot coffee spilling, and lines subjected to sudden strain can cause serious injury. The skipper must do his or her best to alert (or perhaps just remind) every guest to all these hazards on a boat, and be ready with a real first-aid kit and a medical book when trouble arrives.

In the skipper's mind should come first the safety and welfare of the crew, second the safety and welfare of the vessel (where it differs from that of the crew), and third the efficiency of the voyage or race.

Ship's Routine

While most experienced sailors have a good idea of what special rules relating to the personal habits of the crew should be observed on board a vessel, these are different for every boat and for every skipper. The fifty-foot wooden schooner *Mya* was almost lost when a cantaloupe seed jammed her bilge pump open, and for years thereafter her skipper would not permit a cantaloupe on board under any circumstances. Such rules may differ on different types of voyages, too.

Based on bad experiences in the past, a skipper may establish very strict rules on smoking below deck, stowage of personal gear, stowage of cameras or other heavy gear, drinking before a certain hour, talking to whomever has the helm, use of the navigator's station or the charts, handling of expensive or dangerous equipment (loran, the sextant, stove, kerosene lantern), having glassware on deck, or other potentially dangerous practices which may seem harmless to less well-traveled mariners. Such rules may be different for every vessel. The old sailor's wisdom of "different ships, different long splices" still applies.

There may be more idiosyncratic ship's regulations dealing with such things as stowage of seaboots, tidy bunks, opening the icebox for snacks, treatment of wet socks (thrown overboard), potato chips consumed on teak decks, shore shoes carried aboard, etc. These should not be considered on a par with safety regulations, like those suggested above or outlined in many books on the topic; they are rules to make living close together easier. While the skipper has to make all shipboard rules known in advance if they are to be followed scrupulously by all concerned, he has to maintain a fine balance between too many rules and fun. The rules may be posted somewhere below deck, or just mentioned from time to time as needed.

"Happy Hour"

S kippers are always responsible for the safe operation of their vessels, and are therefore responsible for the sobriety of their guests whenever the boat is under way. Heavy drinking and boating have a long and troubled history together, dating to even before the days when dead-drunk sailors were shanghaied from the bar onto a sailing ship, where they awoke the next day far out to sea, on the start of a three-year voyage. Drinking continues to be a problem on the crowded water today; most boating accidents are caused by excessive drinking by the vessels' operators. Drinking is often unwittingly encouraged by the stuffiest of yacht clubs and by the saltiest of sailors, who consider themselves great proponents of safety at sea. Skippers should think long and hard about how much liquor is served to themselves and to the guests on board their yachts.

Note that the new federal policy of Zero Tolerance makes a vessel subject to heavy fines or confiscation by the Coast Guard if illegal drugs in any form are found on board.

The House Gift

N ormally, etiquette would suggest that a guest bring a small gift to the host for the weekend, maybe some wine or an offer to bring a dinner or to buy dinner in a restaurant. Guests and skippers should be aware that the Coast Guard has ruled that gifts to the operator of a vessel, even the purchase of a tank of fuel, may constitute a charter fee, and may subject the vessel to the licensing and operating requirements for "carrying passengers for hire." The fine print in insurance coverage may affect liability in such a case, too. While it probably isn't the intent of the Coast Guard to make all guests arrive for the weekend empty-handed, the skipper and guests might keep this definition of "carrying passengers for hire" in mind.

Clothing

I f you go out in a boat once or twice a year, the chances of having only bathing suits in your duffle when it is blowing a gale and forty degrees, or of having full foulies and gloves when it is baking hot, are good, especially after the skipper has told you to bring only what you will need, and in a small dufflebag. Having the right clothes at the right time on a boat is as chancy as predicting the weather, because it is the same thing.

A marvelous array of new fabrics makes clothing selection a highly subjective and personal matter. You can spend a great deal of money on self-drying, brightly colored, high-tech clothing, from wicking underwear to Arctic hats, breathing storm pants, and fingerless gloves. It has made the chance of being warm and dry and stylish at the same time a high probability.

Clothing is always a topic of much on-board discussion. (The only topics generating more discussion and thought than clothing on a boat are the weather and the food.) Even—or perhaps especially—in the highest levels of offshore competition, one's clothes can become an obsession: what is wet, what is still dry, what is lost in the bilge, what is loaned to every watch, what wears best, what is really waterproof, what is worth the great sums of money spent on it, and what isn't. You might feel you have to spend the money for top-of-the-line, all-weather clothing, and then find that people who go out every weekend have low-tech clothing from ten years ago, and that they don't seem uncomfortable at all. The big racing boats with crews of twenty people often give out complimentary clothing with the boat's name emblazoned on it; while this may be partially for harmony in photographs, it may be more to relieve the crew's mental energy from the strain of discussing the pros and cons of the various types of clothing they each brought aboard, allowing them to concentrate on more important jobs at hand.

The only solid guideline for clothing is that it should be closely guarded, not so much because it might be borrowed as because clothing easily gets out of control on a boat. All clothes, from hats and sunglasses to wet socks and cast-off sweaters, should be carefully stowed and out of sight when not being worn. It may be tempting to ask someone who is going below to hand up your jacket or sunglasses; it may be tempting to stash your sweater in a corner of the cockpit when the sun comes out and then forget about it, but this is how clothing becomes a problem on a boat. Some skippers of the old school used to make a practice of throwing overboard every article of clothing left unattended, to teach the uninitiated to keep their possessions to themselves. This shouldn't be done any more, since even a pair of socks costs as much as a steak, but crew should guard their clothing as though that were still the practice.

Care of the Seasick

I f there were a cure for motion sickness, NASA would have found it for their astronauts. Millions are spent preparing each space-shuttle crew for the rigors of weightlessness, and NASA has probably tried more cures for nausea than are generally available to the boating public, but none has emerged as more effective than others. The nausea, lethargy, and loss of appetite of motion sickness still visit 30 percent of the humans who orbit in outer space. It is the same affliction that visits the weekend sailor crossing the Chesapeake Bay to St. Michaels on a windy Saturday. Even the newest and most high-tech remedy, the medication-releasing round patch worn behind the ear of a sailor the day before departure and throughout the voyage, works only for some people, and sends others into a fantasy land with a dry mouth and a poor idea of which way is up. Then they get sick anyway. Pills, patches, acupressure bracelets, herbs, mantras, crackers—none works as well as lying quietly under a tree. And none works consistently better that the oldest remedies, which include:

A chair suspended from the deckbeam, hanging like a
   canary cage
A gimballed saloon*
Tight corsets to keep the gut from surging
Colonic irrigation
Belladonna plasters over the solar plexus
Constant flow of Champagne

The orator Cicero preferred certain death to seasickness. He had taken refuge from Poplius (Marc Anthony's sicair), who had placed a price on his head, on a vessel, but he preferred to jump overboard and swim ashore into the hands of his enemies, and was assassinated. Such may seem to be the only relief for the victim of seasickness.

---

* The *Bessamer*, a 350-foot paddle steamer, was built in England in 1875 with an entire first-class saloon suspended on gimbals in the middle of the ship.

The greatest sailor of all time, Ulysses, had his moments with *mal de mer*, Homer tells us. Lord Nelson suffered with "Heavy seas, sick to death," and a popular America's Cup skipper is known to suffer from it. Seasickness does not exclude one from the ranks of the finest sailors the world has ever known. What might exclude you from these ranks is a failure in your ability to carry on in spite of the discomfort of nausea. The sailor who honestly admits to occasional bouts of seasickness, but who knows he or she can do the job nonetheless, is far preferable a crewmember than the sailor who swears to never suffer any nausea; the boaster may never have been tested, and may be the one to lie in the cockpit or a bunk and groan while others take over the watch.

Seasickness makes you lethargic, weak, down at the mouth, and hopeless, in addition to dizzy and prone to vomit. It makes you want to roll through the lifelines and slip into the waves to end the horrible condition that flesh is heir to. You may not care if the fuel needs checking, the sails need trimming, or the navigation needs updating. It can make you furious with yourself for being out there at all; so furious that you don't care if you are wet and cold, hungry and dehydrated, or drifting into harm's way.

Neophyte victims of seasickness need care and attention; though they may not get it if things are really rough. Never ask someone with a pale face if he or she feels sick; you can tell by the frown and quiet nature, if not by the sudden trip to the lee rail (the rail that is down, and downwind). Sometimes just thinking about seasickness can rock the boat just a bit more and cast the victim into a sea of despair. People who are seasick should be encouraged to participate actively in whatever is going on on deck, encouraged to drink something (soda or broth is best), and to eat something bland, even if it comes up later. Give the seasick an active job on deck, such as trimming a sail, steering, or watching for a buoy. The less said about being seasick, the better. If the wolf of *mal de mer* knocks on the door, pretend that you do not hear. If you answer the door, the wolf will come bounding in.

If trouble looks inevitable, direct the seasick crew to the lee rail.

Often they will feel much better after a few moments leaning over the rail and clearing out the stomach, and will soon be ready to get on with their duties. Give them a moistened paper towel and a very small glass of water. This small courtesy has a surprisingly helpful effect in bringing the victim's spirits up quickly.

If someone's really in the grip of the wolf and feels unable or unwilling to help manage the vessel, you must send him or her off watch, to a bunk below and amidships (the most comfortable part of the boat) to lie down with a blanket. Once down, though, it may be harder than ever to return to the deck. Stricken crew may say they feel more comfortable huddled in the corner of the cockpit, under a blanket, staring out at the unbalanced horizon, but they get in the way of active crew there, and should be encouraged to wait out their suffering down below, with their eyes closed. It will be warmer, quieter, and easier to get some curative sleep. Lee cloths or leeboards should be set up for sick crew to keep them from tumbling out of the berth in the roll of the waves, but sick crew either forget or don't know what lee cloths are, or what might be the most comfortable berth for them, so the skipper or another active crew member should help to get the sufferer comfortable and safely tucked away.

Plutarch, in his *Treatise on Natural Causes,* said that sleep, either natural or artificial, is the best antidote for *mal de mer* because it relieves the mind of its burden of fear. While not many experienced sailors or scientists would agree that fear is the only cause of seasickness, Plutarch was right about sleep. If the vessel can be operated without them, let the sick crew go to sleep: Send them below and pack them into a berth for the duration of the bad weather. Oral medication may stay down and be more effective when accompanied by a heavy dose of sleep. Even the sickest neophyte may feel better at the next watch.

If the watch below has enjoyed a pleasant sleep, a critical transition occurs when they are called on deck to relieve the on-watch. The brief minutes between lying warm and rested with eyes closed and reaching the deck all dressed and ready for action can be rough moments for any stomach. Anything that the skipper can do before the voyage to speed those seconds will be appreciated by crew making the difficult dash between bunk and deck: snacks to grab from the galley on the way up, for instance, or special stowage areas for things like boots, flashlights, harnesses, or other items that might make the watch on deck more comfortable and safe. Trying to get any task accomplished below deck is sure to worsen whatever queasy feelings someone already has—the less time spent fiddling with things below deck, the better the chance for active recovery.

The skipper might consider a slight change of course or speed to relieve the problems for the crew. Sometimes a very small course adjustment can change a boat's angle to the seas and moderate her motion, perhaps in the lee of an island, or a bit off the wind. A slightly slower speed can ease the pounding of the hull and allow the boat to glide more comfortably over the seas. Though not always possible, such considerations can make the voyage a great deal more pleasant and safe, and not necessarily any longer in the end.

If seasickness continues, it quickly becomes a medical problem and must be taken very seriously indeed. While people don't die of seasickness, they can die of dehydration associated with it. If the victim of seasickness lies below in a seeming coma, oblivious to the activity on deck for over a day, the skipper should consider the person ill, and in need of care and attention. Consult a medical book. It is part of the skipper's job to keep the crew's welfare uppermost in mind and to do everything possible to hasten the end of the trial by waves and bring on the return of good health.

Often enough, when the boat rounds the breakwater and begins to steady her motion in flat water, the sick will rise from their bunks and feel miraculously better, hungry for missed lunches and full of the energy they have built up sleeping, while the other crew members are exhausted from the extra work they have put in. Most people forget their misery entirely after eating a little something. The boat can be cleaned up and a real meal contemplated. Seasickness is perhaps the only disease from which full recovery is just about guaranteed (eventually), though it seems to have a side effect of mild amnesia. That is why people return to sea even after suffering a cruel bout of seasickness, during which they swear never to go near a boat again; they quickly forget how bad it feels to be seasick.

CHAPTER EIGHT

BOAT MAINTENANCE

The condition in which a boat is kept by her owner is an important part of boating etiquette. Surprisingly, a boat's appearance need not be a function of the dollars spent on her at the boat yard, although that helps a good deal. Here is a checklist of details that might be considered by the owner who loves his or her boat and wishes to show the boat off to the greatest advantage at all times.

The Hull

A clean and bright hull might be the first indication of a boat's true nature. Faded dark colors on a fiberglass hull make an otherwise fine yacht look tired and unkempt. On a wooden boat, the seamless glossy coat of paint makes the boat look like she is on her way up, whether the garboards are spongy or not. Glass boats might need a new gelcoat after several years; even white hulls lose their shine eventually. Annual waxing and frequent wipe downs with a mild cleaner keep the hull gleaming from week to week. If your engine exhaust outlet leaves a stain along the hull from drips or exhaust fumes, wipe the hull down frequently, especially after a long day under power, to keep it from getting permanently stained.

On inland passages, where boats churn through the rich, brown swamp waters, a telltale brown "moustache," or bow-wave stain, appears along the waterline at the bow. You can spot boats that have made the long trip up or down the Intracoastal Waterway by the "Waterway smile" they wear at the bow. That moustache is OK while you are making the trip, but when you get where you are going give the boat a "haircut and a shave" to indicate that you have "arrived" after a long trip. The brown stain will make a permanent mark on the gelcoat if left on too long. Oddly enough, blue toilet-bowl cleaner seems to take this stain off neatly without harming the gelcoat or paint underneath.

When the aged leaky steel hull of the J-boat *Endeavour* was pulled from her mud berth of forty years, the first thing the owner, John Amos, did after securing the leaks was to slap a coat of paint on the rough topsides: Endeavour Blue, the color named for the original color of the boat in 1934. This was to signify that the boat had come alive again, and indeed she had.

The single best thing you can do for your boat's appearance is to make the hull shiny and bright.

The Waterline and Boottop

The colored band around the boat just above the surface of the water on the hull is called the waterline, and the second decorative band of another color (if there is one) is called the boottop. Even sitting at the dock, the waterline and boottop will pick up a brown scumline, a bathtub ring of harbor dirt. But these bands are usually of a harder type of paint, so they can withstand abrasive scrubbing. Boat owners should take advantage of this feature and scrub the waterline and boottop frequently with a stiff brush or abrasive pad.

Deck and Cabin

T eak decks are not absolutely necessary in order for a vessel to be considered a "yacht," but they help. Care of teak decks remains a topic of debate among the most knowledgeable charter skippers and big-yacht owners. To scrub or not to scrub, whether to keep the teak golden and oiled with biannual chemical cleaning and scrubbing (and eventual deterioration of the deck) or to leave them "bone," a weathered gray, with eventual drying and cracking of the wood. For teak decks to look their very best, they will take as much work as varnished surfaces. A large expanse of such a deck is a wonder to behold, particularly if you have tried to maintain one in its oiled and golden condition.

Just as teak decks are not really required on a boat, neither is the bright gold teak color mentioned above. The deck can be cleaned when necessary, at least once a year, and allowed to weather evenly without getting too gray or too dry. Mud brought aboard by the anchor or from shore on shoes should be hosed away before it dries in the grain, and grease from spilled food or repair projects should be rinsed out with a teak cleaner and flushed with water. Teak oil can be applied to protect the wood from drying out. The teak will retain all its nonskid properties indefinitely, and look shipshape for many years.

For boats with nonteak decks, there is no excuse for anything but a sparkling clean deck. Hose it with water, fresh or salt, and scrub the waterways. Keep the scuppers or deck drains free of leaves and shells from the mud brought aboard by the anchor. Rough deck surfaces, intended to keep the crew from slipping, collect dirt; they need special attention with a brush if they are not to look like a brown repair patch on the white deck.

Cabin sides don't get very dirty in the course of a season so they tend to be ignored. Keep an eye out for "tear stains" in the cabin from the portholes. Keep the portholes themselves wiped clean with fresh water and a soft cloth if they are easily scratched Plexiglass™, particularly if they are large and afford a view from below. White salt residue makes the surfaces dull.

Clutter

O n long voyages, many sailors like to lash extra equipment all over the deck and cabin top: gerry cans of extra fuel and water, coiled lines, sails, awnings, dinghies, sailboards, etc. At the dock, boats acquire folding chairs, buckets for fishing or beachcombing, uncoiled water hoses, hanging black shower bags, and bicycles. The whole boat begins to look like a backyard full of discarded gear. This is questionable seamanship (a big sea can carry off this heavy gear along with the lifelines it is tied to), and there is no question that extra gear lying around the deck detracts from a boat's appearance. Yacht designers stake their careers and their artistic merit on the careful drawing of a yacht's sheerline. It is too bad if the proud owner then clutters it up by storing gear on the deck and festooning the lifelines with major equipment. A boat should be "clean" in the largest sense of the word, the decks "clear for running," and the curve of the sheer and of the cabin uncluttered.

Awnings and Covers

A wnings should be taut and as close to horizontal as possible. A droopy sunshade makes the whole boat look as though it were melted by the sun. A breeze will catch a loose awning and shake it mercilessly until it rips or tears out its grommets. A tight, well-fitted awning will withstand more wind (though perhaps not a gale) because there is no loose, flapping material subject to a sudden gust. Most sail-boat awnings set best when hoisted and tensioned fore and aft then secured at the edges and corners evenly. This should avoid the dog-house look of the awning peaked in the center.

Sail covers are necessary to protect the sail from the ultraviolet rays of the sun whenever the sails are left unused in bright sunlight. While sail covers may be made to fit snugly or loosely around the furled sail according to the sailmaker's style, they should be stretched tightly fore and aft with as few vertical or diagonal stretch-marks as possible. This assures that the after end of the furled sail is covered and protected.

Ship's Laundry

B oats generate a tremendous amount of laundry, from wet towels to blue jeans that never dry because of the salt in them. When a sunny day comes along, it is tempting to hang out all the ship's laundry, all the towels and foul-weather gear that need air. Lifelines seem to be made to string up clothing, and a certain amount of public airing of the laundry may have to be done, but it is a terrible thing to do to a boat's appearance on an otherwise lovely day. Besides, clothes have a way of drying slowly all day, then just as they dry, flying away and landing in the water. Hang things below and allow a breeze to blow through to dry them on the good days when the crew will all be up on deck. Send everything out to the laundry right from the marina or yacht club; it comes back the same day, all dry and neatly folded. The boat's appearance has not suffered a bit.

Garbage Disposal

P raise and congratulations are due to the crew that totes lots of garbage bags ashore after a short cruise. It means that the garbage did not go over the side into the bay.

In the old days a vessel could return from months at sea with nary a garbage bag to tote ashore. Now even a very small boat returns from a weekend trip with several large plastic bags of refuse. While marinas may grumble as they order larger dumpsters, mariners should be thankful that the garbage is not circulating around the cruising waters.

Unless you spend a great deal of time at sea, far from land, you should bring everything back to the dock with you. Follow the old rule of wilderness camping: What you carry in, you carry out. This applies first and foremost to plastic of any kind. Styrofoam coffee cups, beverage-can rings, plastic packaging, and plastic soda bottles last far longer than you will, and they don't just visually pollute; they kill wildlife for years when discarded in the open. Don't use these items on board, or if absolutely necessary, plan to load them off the boat into dumpsters ashore.

Glass bottles, aluminum cans, and paper garbage—routinely cast overboard when the vessel is way out at sea—do not present the same environmental debacle that plastic presents. But this type of garbage should never be jettisoned when you are anywhere near land. Bob Ballard was disgusted to see a fresh beverage can lying on the bottom of the North Atlantic, at twelve thousand feet, when he discovered the wreck of the *Titanic*. The can was from his own vessel, in defiance of ship's rules.

Organic material is also routinely thrown overboard: dinner scrapings, mildewed fruit, stale bread. Usually it makes fine chum for sea-gulls and ducks, and later for fish and other marine life, but too often such refuse finds its way to shore, where it fouls a beach or lays up alongside another boat. Think carefully before discarding any organic material, even bread crumbs. How would you feel if that material washed up alongside your boat, or lay on your waterfront property, rotting slowly and drawing flies?

Marine Sanitation

The matter of marine sanitation is an important one for a book on boating etiquette to address. It is a matter of common decency and courtesy to comply with the law, and with the intent of the law. While not well understood, or even discussed in yachting circles, sewage disposal is a matter of growing urgency in the marine world. Technology does not permit an ideal solution to the problem of sewage disposal on boats (or on land for that matter) and as a result, even the most environmentally conscientious skipper may have thought up a list of excuses for not installing or not using installed equipment for sewage disposal on board. Instead of thinking up excuses, a concerned skipper might try to think up ways to improve compliance with the law and to speed up technological development of on-board treatment systems so that safe, economical, odor-free, and practical sewage systems become the standard in the marine commu-nity. Keep in mind that some communities, such as the towns of New Shoreham (controlling Great Salt Pond on Block Island), Cuttyhunk, Avalon on Catalina Island, and many on the Great Lakes are prepar-ing to restrict their waters to boats with holding tanks only. For a group of people who appreciate the beauties and cleanliness of the marine environment, mariners are very slow to clean up their own house, and thus lead the way in the nation's concern for clean water.

CHAPTER NINE

SHIP'S DAILY ROUTINE

F irst thing in the morning: start water for coffee. Turn off the riding light if at anchor. In fair weather, wipe brightwork (all varnished wood and polished brass) with a chamois cloth and the available dew. Check anchor rode or mooring pennant and freshen the nip (i.e., adjust the pennant or rode a few inches so that any small cut or pressure on the line at the chock is relieved). Inspect tenders alongside or astern for rainwater or leaks. Bail if necessary. Wipe down the hull with a damp, soapy sponge, or swab the decks with a mop and sea water. Open the hatches and portholes for ventilation. Calculate weather and tides and begin charting a course for the day.

At 8 A.M. raise colors at the cannon's report, first the ensign on the stern, followed by the personal signal and/or the club burgee at the masthead(s), or at the bow on a powerboat. On holidays, the code flags are raised to encircle the boat and dress ship. On Sundays, the Union Jack is raised (stars pointing up) over the foredeck. The Union Jack and the code flags are all brought down before getting under way. Breakfast may be well along, depending on the day's plan. Breakfast dishes should be put away before any open water is encountered.

Throughout the day under way, the skipper is constantly mindful of the presence of other boats and their relative position in his or her boat's course. Whenever a risk of collision is present, the appropriate Rules of the Road come into play, and the skipper decides which boat is the give-way vessel, and which the stand-on vessel. If a change of the course is required by the Rules, the change made is both significant and early, so that all boats in the vicinity understand the action. Whistle signals are used whenever appropriate: One blast signals a turn to starboard, and two blasts signal a turn to port when under power. If traveling in inland waters, these signals are answered by the same signal when understood and agreed to by the approaching boat.

Speed and wake are kept way down whenever other boats may be affected. Powerboats drop down from cruising speed when passing other boats or when entering congested waters. Racing fleets are avoided as a whole; tugs and commercial ships are avoided long before a right-of-way situation develops. Active fishing vessels are avoided, with special consideration given to their nets and lines.

When within range, a VHF radio call can be made to the day's destination, perhaps a marina or harbormaster. Before keying the mike, the skipper listens on the predetermined channel for any radio traffic. The marina or harbormaster may be talking to another boat, but the skipper waits until they are finished before trying to raise them, to let them know his or her ETA and the boat's needs.

Approaching the marina, the skipper discusses the docking maneuver with the crew, detailing the location of the fenders, the most critical lines ashore, and safety precautions, such as not using your feet to fend off the pier. On the approach, if the skipper has nothing further to tell the crew members, who are standing by with lines coiled and ready to throw, he or she can concentrate on calculations of the current, the wind, and the throttle.

With the boat secured at the dock, the departing crewmembers help in a whirlwind cleanup of the vessel below decks, wiping down the head and galley and sweeping the sole. Sails are folded and put away. Sail covers and awnings are set up taut. The boat is hosed down and cleaned as needed. Garbage is taken ashore in sealed bags and deposited in a dumpster. The skipper completes arrangements with the dockmaster or marina office.

At sundown, the flags are brought down from the masthead and off the stern. Sundown is marked by a local cannon report or is determined by consulting a table of sunsets in an almanac or local newspaper. Docklines are checked again to determine the effect of the tidal rise and fall. Hatches are closed against the cool night air and the weather report is reviewed again, for the chance of a storm or rain.

CHAPTER TEN

THE YACHT-CLUB CRUISE

P lanning for the yacht club's summer cruise begins almost a year before the first rendezvous on the water, when the officers of the club hash out an itinerary for the week of cruising. The club officers must plan to visit harbors other than those visited the previous year, commodious enough for their entire fleet (which could be two hundred boats), and hospitable enough to service the needs of perhaps two thousand people on the move. Shore transportation, car parking, groceries, hardware, access to medical facilities, and shoreside accommodations, as well as fuel docks and repair services, must be available. Local yacht clubs, marinas, and harbormasters will have much to say about the fleet's intended visit in their harbor. Scheduling must not conflict with local events, other clubs' cruises, or holidays.

Harbors are selected with sufficient depths for the club's largest boats, requiring maybe ten feet at low water, and with swinging room in the anchorage for 150-footers. They must be sufficiently close that even the small boats can move quickly and safely on to the next harbor in fog or severe weather. And the cruise must be sufficiently scenic or interesting to attract the membership to join it in the first place. Although called a cruise, most such annual outings include a heavy schedule of racing every day, usually point-to-point races to help the fleet get quickly from one harbor to the next. Most of the fleet joins the races daily.

The event may begin with the Captain's Meeting on Friday at 1800 hours; captains only are expected to attend. The commodore gives some welcoming remarks and any news, and introduces local dignitaries or host-club commodores, who also make some remarks. Cautionary notices, scratch sheets, and a hefty booklet are distributed to each captain. The fleet roster gives each boat's name and hailing port, the owner's name, the names of the entire crew (this could be twenty-eight names), and the boat's rating according to a United States Racing Union Racing Certificate supplied by the owner. A big cocktail party begins right after, with old friends from previous years meeting again, greetings to the arriving crew, and the loading of cartons of supplies.

This is a busy time for launches that shuttle people to and from the yachts assembled in the harbor. The launches may be local boats chartered for the event or the club's own launches, brought along for the duration of the cruise. The launch drivers are busy responding to requests for service on the VHF radio and watching for code flag Tango flying from a starboard spreader, indicating a request for transport. New yachts in the fleet are ogled and inspected, old regulars are remembered for their winning ways, their great beauty, or their recent mishaps. This is the time to have your boat all spruced up; for some yachts, this is their finest hour: gleaming bright and clean, in racing trim (as far as possible with all the stores for a full crew for a week aboard), sail covers bent on tight, and flags snapping. No orange jerry cans of extra water tied to the lifelines, no stains dripping from the rusting chainplates, no moustache under the bow from the swamp water of the Intracoastal Waterway, and no laundry drying on the boom. All boats have clean waterlines, their teak decks are golden, and their varnishwork glistens an even color gold. At another time she might have baggywrinkles and banana stalks in the rigging and sailboards on the foredeck. Now she appears as though posing for her formal portrait on the cover of a magazine, clean and neat, gear stowed away, flags flying. And always she should be able to add grace and splendor to whatever harbor she visits. Which is one of the things a good boat should do best, on the yacht-club cruise or not.

The boat manufacturers, dealers, and designers appear in their newest creations, eager to show off their boat's cruisability, racing ability, or good looks. While they don't put up the bright logo banners in the rigging as they do at the boat shows, they make their presence known to those around who might be interested in seeing the new boat. Raft-ups, cockpit gams, and visiting in general begin in earnest.

Colors are observed whether or not the captain is aboard the yacht. At sunset and the report of the cannon on the flagship (the commodore's vessel) or from the clubhouse, the owner's signal and the club burgee are brought down from their masthead locations on every boat, and the national flag is brought in from the stern. Courtesy flags on foreign vessels are left flying under the starboard spreader. (No U.S. registered boat should fly the U.S. flag under the starboard spreader at any time.) The fastidious traditional boat might raise her Night Hawk, to give the crew a wind indicator aloft throughout the night. All vessels at anchor raise and light the riding, or anchor, light.

Parties ashore and aboard may continue for much of the night but in the morning all boats observe colors promptly at 8 A.M., at the flagship's report (no cannons on Sunday). At 8:30, the yachts of each flag officer of the club raise in concert the signal flags indicating the day's destination. The flagship may also announce on a predetermined VHF channel: "The fleet should be advised that the flagship is flying code flags Echo Kilo Uncle Golf." The skipper of each boat in the fleet has to thumb through the club yearbook to see that EKUG means, "The squadron will get under way for Stonington, Connecticut." When each yacht has deciphered the message, she raises her answering pennant (part of every code-flag set) to the starboard spreader to indicate that she has understood the commodore's signals.

Then the parade begins. No vessel precedes the flagship out of the harbor. Your anchor is up and secured, dinghies are aboard, and the engine is on, but you wait courteously for first the flagship, then the other flag-officers' vessels to pass in order of rank before you fall in behind the lead boats. The fleet follows in a disorderly file. On foggy mornings, which you often find at such an hour, it can be very helpful to follow other boats along, especially since they are going to the same place. If it is too foggy or stormy to start a race, the flagship may fly code flag Lima, meaning simply, "Follow me." Usually, the fleet proceeds to the starting line for the race of the day; the answering pennant is doused.

At the starting line, the race committee begins its work of evaluating the weather conditions, anchoring for the starting sequence, and establishing the first leg of the course. All flags on boats planning to race come down, except the class flags attached to the backstay. Spectator boats leave all their flags flying, indicating that they do not plan to race. They stay clear of the boats' maneuvering and racing, and proceed at will to the destination of the day.

Racing takes up the best part of the day. Courtesies are observed during the race that you might expect from people who will be spending the next five consecutive days in friendly proximity, and who have been racing against each other for perhaps several years. Large boats might pass other boats in smaller classes to leeward, leaving the smaller boat with clear air. Yachts guilty of fouling another yacht should drop out of the race immediately by leaving the course and raising their flags, before a protest proceeding need be initiated. All yachts should complete the race if they can, even the ones in dead last place. At the end of the race, the apparent winners are congratulated, the losers are challenged to do better tomorrow. These courtesies do not mean that the racing is not as serious as the best sailors in the fleet can make it.

In the evening, before colors (sunset), the race committee delivers the computer-generated race results to each yacht in person. Invitations for parties to be held later in the cruise are also delivered by hand. Rafting, visiting, and partying continue. Yachts may depart the cruise at any time, signaling their departure by hoisting the code flag Whiskey, to indicate, "I intend to leave the fleet," and notifying the fleet captain by VHF radio; in theory, the club officers are looking out for the welfare of every boat in the fleet.

The yachts have to look shipshape despite a week or more of hard use. Exhaust fumes are scrubbed from the topsides if they make a stain, and the hull is kept generally clean, if not polished. Brightwork should be rinsed with fresh water if salt spray dries on it, and windows (on large boats) and brightwork chamoised every morning. Sails are neatly furled every evening, and the jibs are bagged and put away. Awnings are taut and clean.

Halfway into the week's cruise is the scheduled lay day, when the fleet remains at anchor and "dresses ship" from 8 A.M. to sunset. Special races, shore activities, extra provisioning, and visiting between yachts fill the day. The balance of the week continues with racing every day. Awards are not formally given until the club's annual awards ceremony, usually in the fall.

SHIP AND YACHT NAMES

A vessel's name conveys a lot about how the owner thinks of his or her boat. How do you think a boat with a name like *Marauder* will negotiate a crowded channel? Most jokes get old with constant retelling; how does a name like *MAL de MERried* sound after a few years of ownership? How effective will your radio transmissions be to the boat called *Let's Do It!*? ("*Let's Do It!, Let's Do It!, Let's Do It!*, this is *Why Knot?*, come in on channel 68." "*Why Knot?, Let's Do It!*, negative on Channel 68, try 72.")

Choose boat names with care; people often know owners by their boats, and boats by the choice of their names.

The following list of names from the last four centuries is provided to inspire new yacht owners, who may be seeking a name that will wear well over time, and which may even enhance the value of the boat.

Early Names of Ships and Yachts
WITH APPROXIMATE LAUNCH DATES, WHERE KNOWN

Jupiter, Dutch ship, 1639
Constant Reformation, English
    ship, 1648
Royal Charles, English ship, 1660
Henry
Mary
Expedition

Charles, English yacht, 1663
Merlin, English yacht, 1673
Cleveland, English yacht, 1673
Adventure, English ship, 1673
Princess
Revenge
Kitchen, English yacht, 1675

Names of the
First American Squadron of Ships
LAUNCHED IN 1775

Alfred, warship
Andrew Doria, brigantine
Cabot, warship

Columbus, warship
Providence, warship

American Ships in 1776

Baltimore Hero, privateer
Betsy, brigantine
Lady de Graaff, privateer
L'Indien, warship

Randolf, frigate
Ranger, warship
Smack, brigantine

Clipperships of the 1850s

Arrow	Golden Light	Seaman's Bride
Blessing of the Bay	Grey Feather	Stag Hound
Carrier Dove	Herald of the Morning	Stornaway
Celestial	Highflyer	Sultana
Champion of the Seas	Kathay	Sunny South
Chariot of Fame	La Superior	Susquehanna
Dashing Wave	Lightfoot	Three Bells
Expounder	Northfleet	Westward Ho
Flyaway	Ocean Telegraph	Witch of the Wave
Flying Arrow	Pampero	Wylo
Flying Fish	Pride of the Sea	Ziba
Forward Ho	Race Horse	

Names Considered Suitable for Yachts in 1877

Abeona, Goddess who protected voyagers.

Achilles, Bravest and most handsome of the Greeks.

Avosit, A long-legged bird.

Bella Donna, Beautiful woman.

Bellona, Goddess of war and a charioteer.

Circe, Daughter of the sun.

Corrina, Poetess of Thebes.

Czarina, Empress of Russia.

Daedalus, Inventor of masts and sails for ships, in addition to the well-known wings.

Dione, Ocean nymph.

Duen, Master.

Fortuna, Goddess of happiness and misery.

Gemma, Jewel.

Griffon, Creature with the head and paws of a lion, and the body and wings of an eagle.

Hotspur, Fiery.

Ivanhoe, Title character in Sir Walter Scott's novel of twelfth-century England.

Jaseur, Talker, chatterer.

Juno, Queen of heaven.

Minotaur, Mythological figure, half man, half bull.

Nada, Nothing, a term of endearment.

Nikoma, Victory

Nimrod, The first great hunter.

Nooya, Silver gull of Canada.

Norna, German sea nymph.

Oberon, King of the fairies in medieval folklore and Shakespeare's *A Midsummer Night's Dream*; one of the five satellites of Venus.

Onda, Wave.

Ondina, Little wave.

Paragon, Something excellent.

Phosphorus, Morning star.

Piccola, Little one.

Pomona, Godess of fruit trees.

Queen Mab, Fairy queen who rules dreams of men; poem by Shelley.

Saphaedra, Goddess of tides and currents.

Satanella, Small female devil.

Speranza, Hope.

Sylph Graceful nymph.

Syren, Singing sea nymph.

Titania, Queen of fairies; wife of Oberon in *A Midsummer Night's Dream*; one of five satellites of Uranus.

Una, Heroine of legend.

Undine, Water sprite.

• **Vacuna**, The goddess of leisure and repose.

Vanda, Polish princess.

Varuna, Mythical deity.

Vera, True.

Verve, Dash, spirit.

Virago, Female warrior; bold, furious woman.

Volage, Fickle, inconstant.

Vol-au-Vent, Fly to windward.

Vril, The new force.

Waveny, A river.

Welle, Wavė.

Zamba, Wild doglike animal with horse's head.

Zenobia, Courageous and beautiful queen of Palmyra who led 700,000 men into battle.

Zephyrina, Female version of the west wind.

Zigan, Gypsy.

Names of Early Ocean-Racing Yachts

The following list of ocean racers—through 1946—gives the names of yachts that were well known at the time. Many are still known by knowledgeable sailors of today for various reasons. Many are still sailing under their original names.

Actaea, 61-foot Stephens cutter
Ailsa, 127-foot Fife yawl
Alcyone, 40-foot Casey yawl
Amaryllis, 63-foot yawl
Amberjack, 41-foot Alden schooner
Amorita, 99-foot Smith schooner
Apache, 198-foot Reid bark
Asta, 88-foot Watson yawl
Astarte, 76-foot Herreshoff ketch
Atlantic, 185-foot Gardner schooner
Avanti, 55-foot Stephens yawl
Ayesha, 46-foot Rhodes yawl, still sailing
Baccarat, 46-foot Pouliot cutter
Bagherra, 65-foot Crowninshield schooner
Barlovento, 64-foot Cox and Stevens schooner
Baruna, 72-foot Stephens yawl, still sailing
Belisarius, 54-foot Herreshoff yawl, still sailing
Benbow, 71-foot Clark sloop
Blitzen, 55-foot Stephens cutter, still sailing

Bloodhound, 63-foot Nicholson yawl
Blue Goose, 70-foot Hand schooner
Blue Water, 55-foot Alden schooner
Brilliant, 61-foot Stephens schooner, still sailing
Cambria, 108-foot Ratsey schooner
Caroline, 64-foot Lawley schooner
Chubasco, 67-foot Stephens yawl, still sailing
Coronet, 133-foot Poillon schooner, extant
Curlew, 65-foot Alden schooner
Cygnet, 58-foot Cox and Stevens schooner
Dauntless, 120-foot schooner
Dervish, 85-foot Crane schooner
Diablo, 60-foot Herreshoff schooner
Dorade, 52-foot Stephens yawl, still sailing
Dragoon, 66-foot Ford and Payne ketch
Edlu, 68-foot Stephens yawl, still sailing

Elena, 136-foot Herreshoff schooner
Elizabeth McCaw, 63-foot Stephens yawl
Enchantress, 136-foot Smith schooner
Endymion, 135-foot Crane schooner
Escapade, 72-foot Rhodes yawl, still sailing
Fandango, 84-foot Burgess schooner
Fearless, 54-foot Alden schooner
Foxhound, 63-foot Nicholson cutter
Gesture, 57-foot Stephens sloop, still sailing
Golden Eye, 41-foot Rhodes yawl, still sailing
Good News, 64-foot Stephens yawl, extant
Grenadier, 59-foot Alden schooner
Guinevere, 195-foot Swasey schooner
Gypsy, 50-foot Paine sloop, still sailing
Hallowe'en, 70-foot Fife cutter, still sailing
Hamburg, Watson schooner
Hamrah, 54-foot ketch
Hawaii, 70-foot Crowninshield schooner
Henrietta, 107-foot schooner
Highland Light, 62-foot Paine cutter, still sailing
High Tide, 70-foot Alden schooner
Hokuloa, 36-foot Alden sloop, still sailing

Hother, 46-foot Rhodes cutter, still sailing
Ilex, 50-foot Nicholson yawl
Islander, 34-foot yawl
Isolt, 62-foot Burgess cutter
Jolie Brise, 56-foot Paumelle cutter
Kirawan, 53-foot Rhodes cutter
Ladona, 81-foot Hand schooner
Landfall, 71-foot Herreshoff ketch, still sailing
Land's End, 38-foot Crocker ketch, still sailing
Latifa, 69-foot Fife yawl, still sailing
Lexia, 64-foot Shepherd cutter
Lurline, 86-foot Turner schooner
Magic Carpet, 38-foot Atkin ketch
Maid of Maltham, 48-foot Giles cutter
Malabar, various Alden schooners to 58 feet, many still sailing
Malay, 45-foot Roue schooner
Mandoo, 71-foot Alden schooner
Mariner, 107-foot Burgess schooner
Maruffa, 67-foot Rhodes yawl
Mary Ann, 41-foot Alden schooner
Memory, 59-foot Herreshoff cutter
Meridian, 72-foot Alden schooner
Merry Widow, 52-foot Alden schooner
Miladi, 32-foot Herreshoff cutter
Mist, 38-foot Lawley schooner
Mistress, 60-foot Hoyt schooner
Mohawk, 60-foot Alden schooner
Mustang, 45-foot Stephens sloop, still sailing

Nam Sang, 66-foot Paine ketch
Narwhal, 40-foot Rhodes cutter
Navigator, 78-foot Burgess schooner
Neith, 52-foot Herreshoff cutter,
still sailing
Nimrod, 44-foot Casey yawl
Nina, 59-foot Burgess schooner,
still sailing
Nordlys, 71-foot Roue schooner
Nordwind, 78-foot Gruber yawl
Northern Light, 45-foot Roue
schooner
Patience, 68-foot Nicholson cutter
Peter von Danzig, 59-foot Gruber
yawl
Pinta, 57-foot Alden schooner
Restless, 40-foot Lawley schooner
Revenoc, 45-foot Stephens sloop
Rofa, 50-foot Herreshoff schooner
Roland von Bremen, 58-foot Gruber
yawl
Rose of Sharon, 52-foot Burgess
schooner, stillsailing
Rugosa, 59-foot Herreshoff yawl
Santana, 55-foot Stephens schooner
Scaramouche, 41-foot Schock
schooner
Seafarer, 91-foot Crowninshield
schooner
Sea Witch, 54-foot Alden yawl
Señora, 70-foot Mower schooner
Skal, 48-foot Rhodes cutter
Spookie, 45-foot Stephens cutter
Starlight, 44-foot Stephens cutter
Stella Maris, 54-foot Steele ketch
Stiarna, 63-foot Nicholson cutter

Stormy Weather, 53-foot
Stephens yawl, still sailing
Suluan, 44-foot Luders yawl
Sunbeam, 157-foot Byrne schooner
Surprise, 44-foot McManus
schooner
Svaap, 32-foot Alden ketch
Talayha, 102-foot Herreshoff cutter
Tamerlane, 38-foot Huntington
yawl
Teal, 53-foot Alden schooner
Teragram, 58-foot Alden schooner
Thistle, 150-foot Wintringham
schooner
Tigress, 56-foot Hand schooner
Trade Wind, 57-foot Alden schoon-
er, still sailing
Tradition, 60-foot Alden schoon-
er, still sailing
Two Brothers, 43-foot Alden
schooner
Utowana, 190-foot Webb schooner
Vagrant, 76-foot Herreshoff
schooner
Valkyrie, 73-foot Alden ketch
Vamarie, 70-foot Morgan ketch
Vega, 47-foot Eldridge-McInnis
schooner
Venona, 65-foot Smith schooner
Vesta, 105-foot Alden schooner
Volante, 52-foot Alden schooner
Voyager, 44-foot Stephens yawl
Water Gypsy, 59-foot Alden
schooner
Whistler, 61-foot Hand schooner
Windigo, 71-foot Stephens yawl

Zaida, 57-foot Alden yawl, still
    sailing
Zeearend, 55-foot Stephens yawl

Zodiac, 126-foot Hand schooner
Zoriada, 56-foot Kemp cutter
Zuhrah, 84-foot Lawley schooner

How many of today's yachts' names will be known after more than forty years? Those marked as still sailing or extant may not be the only ones. Research is ongoing.

COMMON MISTAKES IN USAGE

Wrong: "Pass to *port* of the lighthouse."
Right: "Pass to *the south* of the lighthouse" or "Leave the lighthouse to *starboard.*"
Neither a lighthouse, a pier, a buoy, nor a sandbar has a port or starboard side, but they do have a south, north, east, or west side, a windward or leeward side, a seaward side, and a deep-water side. Only a boat has a port and a starboard side.

Wrong: "Put the *bumpers* over the side."
Right: "Put the *fenders* over the side."
Bumpers are on the front of a car; fenders protect the side of a boat.

Wrong: "The boat is at the end of the *dock.*"
Right: "The boat is at the end of the *pier, wharf,* or *float.*"
The dock is where the boat lies; either in the water or in a dry dock. The pier, wharf, or float is where you walk to get on the boat while the boat is in the dock.

Wrong: "We are doing eight *knots per hour*."
Right: "We are doing eight *knots*, or eight *nautical miles per hour*.
The term "knot" is a measure of speed, not of distance. It means "nautical miles per hour."

Wrong: "The *tide* runs at two knots" or "The *tide* was against us."
Right: "The *current* runs at two knots" or "The *current* was against us."
Tides are the rise and fall of the water caused by the gravitational pull of the moon and sun. The tide goes up and down, and generates the current, which flows horizontally.

Wrong: Flying the U.S. flag under the spreader.
The U.S. flag is always flown from the place of highest honor on U.S. registered ships and boats. It is flown between 8 A.M. and sunset.

NEW YORK YACHT CLUB SIGNAL CODE

T he signals in the Yacht Code consist chiefly of signals for inter-communication between vessels of the squadron.

Racing and Special Signals	**D to Z**
Other Racing Signals	**AI to AY**
General Signals	**BA to GT**
Designating Signals	**HA to HN**
Days of the Week	**IQ to IZ**
Hours of the Day	**JA to KY**
Names of Places	**NA to WI**

A yacht signaling another yacht in a Club Code should fly as the first flag in the hoist the Club Burgee of the Club whose Code is being used.

When operating as a squadron, however, the Club Burgee may be dispensed with if so specified by the General Orders or the Sailing Instruction.

A yacht signaling another yacht in the International Code may opt to fly the Code (Answering) Pennant either as the first flag in the hoist or a separate hoist.

No designator is used when signaling merchantmen, naval vessels, etc. in the International code.

When several flag hoists are displayed simultaneously they are to be read in the following order: (a) Masthead, (b) Triatic stay, (c) Starboard yardarm or spreader, (d) Port yardarm or spreader.

When more groups than one are shown on the same halyard, they must be separated by the tackline and be read in the numerical order of their superiority.

When more hoists than one are shown at the same yardarm or spreader, but on different halyards, the outboard hoist is to be read first. When more hoists than one are shown at the triatic stay, the foremost hoist is to be read first.

A signal is said to be superior to another when hoisted before, either as regards time or hoist. It is said to be inferior when it is after, either in point of time or hoist.

All vessels to which signals are addressed shall hoist the Code (Answering) Pennant partially (at the dip) as soon as each signal is observed, and full up (two-blocked) when such signal is understood.

The signal of execution for all signals is the hauling down of the signals.

When additional signals are needed, they will be authorized by general orders and should be entered in club books.

See H. O. 102 for proper procedure in making signals and for complete Emergency and International Codes

Racing and Special Signals

D	Do you assent to postponing the race until later in the day?
E	Do you assent to calling the race off for the day?
T	Send Club Launch.
W	Permission to leave squadron is requested.
X	Permission to proceed at will is requested.
Y	Leave all marks to starboard.
Z	Leave all marks to port.

Other Racing Signals

A I   Finish—This yacht will take time at finish.
A J   Finish—Will you take time at finish?
A K   Finish—Yachts will take their own time at finish.
A N   Race Committee—Is Committee on Board Committee boat?
A O   Race Committee—Report is ready.
A P   Race Committee—Report on board this vessel at —.
A Q   Race Committee—Do you agree to race tomorrow?
A V   Start—Race will be sailed on —.
A W   Start—Race will be sailed today at —.
A X   Start—Race will be sailed tomorrow at —.
A Y   Start—When will race be started?

General Signals

B A   Anchor—Are you going to anchor at —?
B C   Anchor—at —.
B D   Anchor—at will.
B E   Anchor clear of the channel.
B F   Anchor for night at —.
B G   Anchor—intend to anchor during fog.
B H   Anchor near me.
B I   Anchorage should be shifted; you will be aground.
B L   Assistance—Do not require further assistance.
B M   Assistance—Do you require assistance?
B N   Assistance—Do you requre a tow?
B S   Assistance—send anchor.
B T   Assistance—send hawser.
B U   Assistance—send tow boat. (See also "Emergency Signals" for International Code signals requesting assistance.)
C A   Boat(s) adrift—please pick up.

C B Boat(s) from all yachts report to Flagship for instructions.

C D Boat(s) from this yacht return immediately.

C E Boat(s) cannot be sent.

C F Send boat alongside.

C G Send boat ashore.

C H Send boat to Flagship.

C I Boat will be sent for you.

C J Will you send a boat for me?

C P Captains and guests are invited on board Flagship at —.

C Q Captains and guests are invited on board this yacht at —.

C R Captains' meeting will be held on Flagship at —.

C S Captains report on board Flagship on coming to anchor.

C T Captains' meeting will be held on board —.

C U Code—Have no International Code book.

C V Code—Will (or will you) use the International Code Signal?

C W Code—Captains' meeting will be held at —.

C X Colors—Morning colors.

C Y Colors—Evening colors.

C Z Congratulations, well done.

D A Engagement—Previous engagement prevents.

D C Mail for you ashore at —.

D D Mail—Is there mail for me?

D E Mail—Please bring or send mail.

D G Power yachts will take sailing yachts in tow.

D H Power yachts will tow sailing yachts after finish.

D J Signal annulled.

D K Signal cannot be complied with.

D L Signal—Do you understand my signal?

D M Signal for me should be repeated.

D N Signal should be shifted to more conspicuous hoist. (See **ZL** under "Emergency Signals" for "Signal not understood.")

E A Squadron—Anchor at —.

E B Squadron—Divine service will be held on Flagship on Sunday at —.

E C Squadron—disbanded.

E D Squadron—disbands at —.

E F   Squadron—disbands on —.
E G   Squadron—dress ship at —.
E H   Squadron—dress ship at colors on —.
E I   Squadron—get underway.
E J   Squadron—get underway at —.
E K   Squadron—get underway for —.
E L   Squadron—get underway tomorrow at —.
E M   Squadron—illuminate on night of —.
E O   Squadron—not to get underway at present.
E P   Squadron—not to get underway today.
E Q   Squadron—Proceed at will.
E R   Squadron—Proceed at will to —.
E S   Squadron—Will join the squadron at —.
E T   Squadron—Will you join the squadron at —.
F A   Supplies—Alcohol is needed.
F B   Supplies—Food is needed.
F C   Supplies—Fuel oil is needed.
F D   Supplies—Garbage boat is needed.
F E   Supplies—Gasoline is needed.
F G   Supplies—Ice is needed.
F H   Supplies—Water is needed.
F I   Taxi—order one taxi cab for me.
F J   Taxi—order two taxicabs for me.
F K   Thank you.
F L   Weather—calm.
F M   Weather—clear.
F N   Weather—foggy.
F O   Weather—heavy wind.
F P   Weather—moderate sea.
F Q   Weather—rough sea.
F R   Weather prediction—Good weather.
F S   Weather prediction—Small yachts should make harbor.
F T   Weather prediction—Stormy weather (from —).
F U   Weather prediction—Watch ground tackle.
F V   What is the weather outside?
F W   What is the weather prediction?

F X   When did you leave — (or pass —)?
F Y   Where are you bound?
F Z   Where are you from?
G A   When do you go ashore?
G B   Will be on board at —.
G C   Will not go ashore.
G D   Will send a reply.
G E   Will you and guests come aboard at —?
G F   Will you and guests breakfast with me at—?
G H   Will you and guests dine with me at —?
G I   Will you and guests lunch with me at —?
G J   Will you come aboard at —?
G K   Will youbrealfast with me at —?
G L   Will you dine with me at—?
G M   Will you lunch with me at —?
G O   Will you meet me ashore at —?
G P   Will you meet me at club at —?
G T   Wish you a pleasant voyage.

Designating Signals

H A	Commodore	H G	Fleet Surgeon
H B	Vice Commodore	H J	Race Committee
H C	Rear Commodore	H K	Club Station
H F	Fleet Captain	H N	Fleet Chaplain

Days of the Week

I Q	Sunday	I V	Friday
I R	Monday	I W	Saturday
I S	Tuesday	I X	Today
I T	Wednesday	I Y	Tomorrow
I U	Thursday	I Z	Yesterday

Hours of the Day

J A	MIDNIGHT	J N	6:00	"	K A	NOON	K N	6:00	"
J B	12:30 A.M.	J O	6:30	"	K B	12:30 P.M.	K O	6:30	"
J C	1:00	"	J P	7:00	"	K C	1:00	"	K P	7:00	"
J D	1:30	"	J Q	7:30	"	K D	1:30	"	K Q	7:30	"
J E	2:00	"	J R	8:00	"	K E	2:00	"	K R	8:00	"
J F	2:30	"	J S	8:30	"	K F	2:30	"	K S	8:30	"
J G	3:00	"	J T	9:00	"	K G	3:00	"	K T	9:00	"
J H	3:30	"	J U	9:30	"	K H	3:30	"	K U	9:30	"
J I	4:00	"	J V	10:00	"	K I	4:00	"	K V	10:00	"
J K	4:30	"	J W	10:30	"	K J	4:30	"	K W	10:30	"
J L	5:00	"	J X	11:00	"	K L	5:00	"	K X	11:00	"
J M	5:30	"	J Y	11:30	"	K M	5:30	"	K Y	11:30	"

Names of Places

[The New York Yacht Club is the only club to have devised a set of signals for place names.]

N A Absecon, N.J.
N B Ambrose Channel Light Tower
N C Annapolis, Md.
N D Atlantic Highlands, N.J.
N E Bakers Island Light, Me.
N F Baltimore, Md.
N G Bangor, Me.
N H Bar Harbor, Me.
N I Bar Island, North side of Bar Harbor, Me.
N J Barnegat Light, N.J.

N K Bath, Me.
N L Bass Harbor, Me.
N M Bay Ridge, N.Y. Bay
N O Beaver Tail, R.I.
N P Belfast, Me.
N Q Beverly, Mass.
N R Black Rock Harbor, Conn.
N S Block Island, R.I., East Harbor
N T Block Island, West Harbor, Great Salt Pond
N U Blue Hill, Me.
N V Brenton Reef Light

N W	Bristol, R.I.	P C	Cuttyhunk, Mass.
N X	Boon Island, Me.	P D	Deer Island Thorofare, Me.
N Y	Boothbay, Me.	P E	Delaware Breakwater, Del.
N Z	Boston, Mass.	P F	Duck Island Breakwater, Conn.
O A	Burnt Coat Harbor, Me.		
O B	Buck Harbor, Me.	P G	Dutch IslandHarbor, R.I.
O C	Buzzards Bay Entrance Light Tower, Mass.	P H	Dyer Bay, Me.
		P I	East Chop, Vineyard Haven, Mass.
O D	Camden, Me.		
O E	Cape Ann, Mass.	P J	Eastern Point Breakwater, Mass.
O F	Cape Charles, Va.		
O G	Cape Cod Canal (East Entrance), Mass.	P K	Eastport, Me.
		P L	Eaton's Neck, N.Y.
O H	Cape Cod Canal (West Entrance), Mass.	P M	Edgartown, Mass.
		P N	Eggemoggin Reach, Me.
O I	Cape Elizabeth, Me.	P O	Egg Rock, Frenchman Bay, Me.
O J	Cape Henlopen, Del.		
O K	Cape Henry, Va.	P Q	Falkner Island, Conn.
O L	Cape May, N.J.	P R	Fire Island Light.
O M	Cape Poge, Mass.	P S	Fishers Island Sound.
O N	Cape Porpoise Harbor, Me.	P T	Flanders Bay, Me.
O P	Cape Sable, N.S.	P U	Franklin Island Light House, Me.
O Q	Captains Island Light, Conn.		
O R	Casco Bay, Me.	P V	Fort Pond Bay, N.Y.
O S	Casco Passage, Me.	P W	Fortress Monroe, Va.
O T	Castine, Me.	P X	Fox Island Thorofare, Me.
O U	Chatham Lights, Mass.	P Y	Gardiners Island, N.Y.
O V	Chatham Roads, Mass.	P Z	Gardiners Bay, N.Y.
O W	City Island, N.Y.	Q A	Gay Head, Mass.
O X	Cold Spring Harbor, L.I., N.Y.	Q B	Gilkey Harbor, Isleboro, Me.
		Q C	Glen Cove, N.Y.
O Y	Clarks Point, Buzzards Bay, Mass.	Q D	Gloucester, Mass.
		Q E	Gloucester, Eastern Point
O Z	Cranberry Island, Me.	Q F	Goat Island, Me.
P A	Cross Rip Shoal Horn Buoy	Q G	Grand Manan, N.B.
P B	Cutler, Little River, Me.	Q H	Grand Manan Channel, N.B.

Q I	Graves, The, Mass.	R T	Mount Desert Rock, Me.
Q J	Gravesend Bay, N.Y.	R U	Mystic Seaport, Conn.
Q K	Greeenport, N.Y.	R V	Nahant, Mass.
Q L	Greenwich, Conn.	R W	National Harbor of Refuge, Del.
Q M	Greens Ledge Light, Nor-walk, Conn.	R X	Nantasket Roads, Mass.
		R Y	Nantucket, Mass.
Q N	Hadley Harbor, Mass.	R Z	Nantucket Shoals Lightship
Q O	Half Way Rock, Mass.	S A	Nauset Beacon, Mass.
Q P	Half Way Rock, Me.	S B	New Bedford, Mass.
Q R	Halifax, N.S.	S C	Newburyport, Mass.
Q S	Hamburg Cove, Conn.	S D	New Haven, Conn.
Q T	Hampton Roads, Va.	S E	New London, Conn.
Q U	Hardings Ledge, Mass.	S F	Newport, R.I.
Q V	Harpswell Sound, N.B.	S G	New Rochelle, N.Y.
Q W	Head Harbor, N.B.	S H	New York, N.Y.
Q X	Highland Light, Mass.	S I	Norfolk, Va.
Q Y	Horseshoe, N.J.	S J	North Haven, Me.
Q Z	Horton Point, N.Y.	S K	Northeast Harbor, Me.
R A	Hudson River, N.Y.	S L	Noyack Bay, N.Y.
R B	Hull, Mass.	S M	Old Field Point Light, N.Y.
R C	Huntington Bay, N.Y.	S N	Orient Harbor, N.Y.
R D	Hyannis Port, Mass.	S O	Orient Point Light, N.Y.
R E	Isleboro, Me.	S P	Oyster Bay, N.Y.
R F	Kittery, Me.	S Q	Padanaram, Mass.
R G	Larchmont Harbor, N.Y.	S R	Pleasant Bay, Me.
R H	Lloyd Harbor, N.Y.	S T	Plum Gut, N.Y.
R I	Mackerel Cove, Me.	S U	Plymouth, Mass.
R J	Manhasset, L.I.	S V	Point Judith, R.I.
R K	Marblehead, Mass.	S W	Point Judith Breakwater, R.I.
R L	Marion, Mass.	S X	Port Clyde, Me.
R M	Mattapoisett, Mass.	S Y	Port Jefferson, N.Y.
R N	Matinecock Point, N.Y.	S Z	Portland, Me.
R O	Monhegan, Me.	T A	Portland Lighted Horn Buoy, Me.
R P	Monomoy, Mass.		
R Q	Montauk Point, N.Y.	T B	Portsmouth, N.H.
R S	Morgan Bay, Me.	T C	Portsmouth, Little Harbor, N.H.

T D	Pretty Marsh Harbor, Me.	U N	Tompkinsville, S.I., N.Y.
T E	Provincetown, Mass.	U O	Trafton Island, Me.
T F	Providence, R.I.	U P	Vineyard Haven, Mass.
T G	Quicks Hole, Mass.	U Q	Watch Hill, R.I.
T H	Race Rock Light, N.Y.	U R	Wellfleet, Cape Cod, Mass.
T I	Race, The, N.Y.	U S	West Chop, Vineyard Haven,
T J	Riverside, Conn.		Mass.
T K	Rockland, Me.	U T	West Harbor, Fishers Island,
T L	Rockport, Me.		N.Y.
T M	Roque Island, Me.	U V	Whitehead Island Light, Me.
T N	Sag Harbor, N.Y.	U W	Wings Neck, Mass.
T O	Sakonnet River, R.I.		(Wenaumet Neck).
T P	Salem, Mass.	U X	Winter Harbor, Me.
T Q	Sandy Hook, N.J.	U Y	Woods Hole, Mass.
T R	Saybrook Breakwater, Conn.	U Z	Wood Island, Me.
T S	Seagirt Light, N.J.	V A	Alexandria Bay.
T U	Seal Island Light, N.S.	V B	(See Emergency Signal.)
T V	Seguin Island, Me.	V C	Buffalo.
T W	Severn River, Md.	V D	Charlotte.
T X	Sheffield Island Light	V E	Chicago.
	House, Conn.	V F	Cleveland.
T Y	Shelter Island, N.Y.	V G	Coburg.
T Z	Shinnecock Light, N.Y.	V H	Country Club.
U A	Small Point Harbor, Me.	V I	Detroit.
U B	Somes Sound, Me.	V J	Duluth.
U C	Southwest Harbor, Me.	V K	Dunkirk.
U D	Southeast Harbor, Me.	V L	Erie.
U E	St. John, N.B.	V M	Georgian Bay.
U F	Stamford, Conn.	V N	Goodrich.
U G	Stonington, Conn.	V O	Green Bay.
U H	Stratford Point Light, Conn.	V P	Hamilton.
U I	Stratford Shoal Light, Conn.	V Q	Harbor Beach.
U J	Swans Island, Me.	V R	Harbor Point.
U K	Tarpaulin Cove, Mass.	V S	Houghton.
U L	Tenants Harbor, Me.	V T	Lake St. Clair Club.
U M	Thimble Islands, Conn.	V U	Mackinac Island.

V W Marquette.
V X Milwaukee.
V Y Nipegon.
V Z Oswego.
W A Port Huron.
W B Presque Isle.
W C Put-in-Bay.

W D Sackets Harbor.
W E Sandusky.
W F Sault Ste. Marie.
W G Toledo.
W H Toronto.
W I Welland Canal.

Emergency Signals

C Yes—(affirmative).
F I am disabled—communicate with me.
N No—(negative).
O Man overboard.
U You are running into danger.
V I require assistance.
A E I must abandon my vessel.
A N I need a doctor.
C B 4 I require immediate assistance; I am aground.
C B 5 I require immediate assistance; I am drifting.
C B 6 I require immediate assistance; I am on fire.
C B 7 I require immediate assistance; I have sprung a leak.
K Q I I am ready to be taken in tow.
N C I am in distress and requre immediate assistance.
Z L Your signal has been received but not understood.

For all other communication with Naval, Coast Guard, or Merchant Vessels, yachts must use the International Code Book (See H.O.102).

GLOSSARY

Aboard in or on a ship or boat

Aloft above the vessel, in the rigging

Anchor rode the rope or chain used to anchor the boat

Anemometer a wind-velocity indicator, usually in the form of three small cups spinning on a vertical spindle

Answering pennant a red and white vertically striped pennant, part of a set of signal flags, hoisted to indicate that a message is understood

Apparent wind the wind as it is perceived on board a boat. It will differ from the true wind by a factor of the boat's speed and course.

Autopilot an electronic compass-related steering aid that maintains a steady course. Sailboats may have a wind-direction sensing component.

Azimuth the BEARING of a celestial body

Backing wind wind changing direction counterclockwise

Backstay a stay supporting the mast from the STERN to the masthead. Running backstays are in pairs (PORT and STARBOARD) and are adjustable with each TACK.

Baggywrinkle fuzzy chafing gear made of old rope, to protect sails from wear and tear against the rig

Bark (barque) a vessel with three masts, square-rigged on the fore and mainmasts, FORE-AND-AFT on the MIZZEN

Barquentine similar to a BARK but FORE-AND-AFT on the main and MIZZEN

Bearing the horizontal angle between two objects. It may be a compass angle or a relative angle.

Beaufort scale a scale of wind conditions in which Force 0 is a flat, glassy calm, and Force 12 is a hurricane

Bend on to rig a sail to mast and boom in preparation for raising the sail

Berth a narrow bed on board a boat

Boottop the second line of color painted around the waterline

Bosun's chair a small seat of canvas or wood used to haul a person ALOFT to inspect or repair rigging or sails

Bow the front end of the vessel

Bow line the dockline that secures the BOW of the boat

Bowline a sailor's favorite knot for making a loop in a LINE; it is strong, easy to untie even after a strain, and it never slips (pronounced bo' lin)

Bowsprit the long spar that extends ahead of the BOW

Breakwater an artificial barrier intended to add protection from heavy seas to harbors or inlets

Bridge the control center on a ship

Brig or **Brigantine** a two-masted vessel, square-rigged on the foremast, FORE-AND-AFT on the mainmast

Brightwork varnished wood or polished brass on deck

Buoy a floating aid to navigation, or a small marking float

Burdened vessel the old term for the GIVE-WAY VESSEL in a right-of-way situation; still used frequently

Burgee a triangular PENNANT or SWALLOW-TAILed flag indicating a vessel's owner or club association

Call sign the group of letters or numbers assigned to a vessel for radio identification

Canton the top, inner corner of a flag

Canvas The general term for all sails set, whether made of canvas or synthetic material

Chafing gear soft wrappings in the rigging to prevent wear and tear on sails or LINE

Chainplates structural supports in the hull for securing the shrouds

Chart a map of the water showing coastline, rocks, BUOYs, and much more

Chock a strong fitting for LINEs passing over the rail

Clean lines an unobstructed visual run of the hull line from BOW to STERN

Cleat a horned fitting used to secure a LINE

Cockpit a well in the deck of a boat where the wheel or tiller is located

Colors the national ENSIGN, often expanded to mean all flags flown with the ensign

Compass course the course steered as indicated by the compass

Current the horizontal movement of water caused by tidal or other forces

Cutter a sailboat with a FORE-AND-AFT mainsail and two or more headsails

Danger signal five or more blasts of a horn or whistle, indicating "Danger! Stop your intentions!"

Depth sounder an electronic depth-measuring instrument

Dip to lower the ENSIGN one-third of the way down the staff to show honor to a warship. *At the dip* indicates a flag one-third of the way down the flagstaff.

Ensign the national flag flown by ships of the nation

Fathom six feet of water

FCC the Federal Communications Commission, the agency governing radio equipment and operation

Fend off to prevent violent contact when coming alongside

Fender a sturdy, inflatable cushion designed to protect the TOPSIDES from rough piers

Fenderboards stout timbers hung horizontally over the side between FENDERs and rough pilings

Flag hoist the position of a flag HALYARD and the flag fully raised, as in the STARBOARD flag hoist, which runs from the deck to a small block attached to the starboard spreader

Fly the longer, horizontal dimension of a flag

121

Fore-and-aft parallel to the centerline of the vessel

Foredeck the section of the deck at the BOW

Forestay the stay supporting the mast, from the BOW to the masthead

Fouled anchor (1) an anchor caught up in rope or another entanglement. (2) part of an official seal of high office in maritime administration.

Gaff a spar to which the upper edge of a four-sided FORE-AND-AFT sail is attached

Gale Force 8 on the BEAUFORT SCALE, with winds from 34 to 40 KNOTs (39 to 46 MPH)

Genoa an oversized, overlapping jib used primarily when sailing upwind

Gilguys light LINEs used to tie unused HALYARDs away from the mast, to avoid chafe

Gimballed suspended on two pivot points or concentric rings to permit an object (a table, a compass, a stove) to remain level in spite of the vessel's motion

Give-way vessel the vessel that must alter course or speed to stay clear of the STAND-ON VESSEL; also called the BURDENED VESSEL

Ground tackle a general term for all the gear associated with anchoring

Growler a piece of low-lying ice floating in the sea

Halyard LINE used to haul a sail or flag ALOFT

Head the toilet or toilet room on a vessel

Helm the steering apparatus or steering characteristics

Hurricane Force 12 on the BEAUFORT SCALE, with winds of 63 KNOTs (73 MPH) or higher

Inland Rules the NAVIGATION RULES used inside demarcation lines at the entrance to most harbors, rivers, bays, and inlets. Similar to the INTERNATIONAL RULES but changed to reflect the smaller size of boats on inland waters.

International Rules NAVIGATION RULES used outside the demarcation lines at the entrance to harbors, rivers, bays, and inlets

Jibe to swing the boom across the boat as the wind direction changes across the STERN

Ketch a two-masted sailboat whose MIZZEN is large and placed forward of the rudderpost

Knot a unit of speed equalling one NAUTICAL MILE per hour

Lee the vessel's side (or the coast) which the wind crosses second

Leech the trailing edge of a FORE-AND-AFT sail

Lee cloth a sturdy cloth laced on the edge of a bunk and attached overhead to prevent a sleeper from rolling out of the bunk in a SEAWAY

Lifelines stout wire (often plastic coated) rigged around the perimeter of the boat to serve as a handrail, and to prevent crew from falling overboard

Line rope, when used aboard a vessel

Long splice a splice joining two rope ends which does not increase the diameter of the rope

Loran (from *long range navigation*) an electronic position-finding receiver

Marconi historical name for the modern triangular mainsail of most sailboats

Mizzen the aftermost mast and sail in a YAWL, KETCH, or FORE-AND-AFT-rigged ship

Morse code a signal code comprising dots and dashes permitting communication by sound or electronic signal

Muscleboat the generic term for a class of large powerboats designed for high speed only, characteristically with an oversize engine, flush deck, and tiny COCKPIT

Nautical mile one minute of latitude, or about 6,080 feet

Navigation Rules the RULES OF THE ROAD in the U.S.

Nip a short turn or twist in a rope

Nun a cylindrical red unlit BUOY, with even numbers

Observance of colors the display of the national ENSIGN and other flags from 8 A.M. to sunset

Off soundings in water so deep that a sounding lead would not touch bottom, usually considered water deeper than 100 FATHOMs

Overtaking vessel the vessel moving faster, and therefore required to give way to the overtaken vessel

123

Pennant a narrow, tapering flag

Pig stick a long, lightweight pole used to raise the BURGEE above the masthead

Port the left side of a vessel, when viewed facing the BOW

Port tack the TACK where the wind crosses the PORT side of a sailboat first; the sails (and boom) are on the STARBOARD side. The port-tack boat is the BURDENED VESSEL and must give way to a boat on the STARBOARD TACK.

Private signal a yacht owner's personal flag, also called the owner's signal or house flag

Privileged vessel the old term for the STAND-ON VESSEL, the vessel with the right-of-way.

Protest a formal objection by one yacht to another yacht's action on the racecourse

Pulpit rigid framework at the BOW supporting LIFELINES

Radar reflector a passive sphere of metal plates that reflect a radar's signals

Relative bearing the BEARING of an object in relation to the vessel's centerline

Riding light the anchor light, a 360° white light shown at night when the vessel is at anchor

Rigging, standing the wire rigging that holds up the mast

Rode the anchor LINE

Rules of the Road a set of requirements to promote safe navigation, including use of navigation lights, steering rules, sound signals, and distress signals. They include the INLAND RULES and the INTERNATIONAL RULES. Also called *72 COLREGS*.

Running Lights the lights required by the NAVIGATIONAL RULES for operating a vessel at night, red on the PORT side, green on the STARBOARD side, plus other appropriate white lights

Sailboard generic term for a sailing surfboard with a small sail held by one person, who is standing on the board

Schooner a vessel with two or more masts, with the foremast shorter than the mainmast

Scope the ratio of the length of the RODE to the depth of the water the anchor is set in

Scuppers drain holes in the deck

Seaway, in a in choppy or heavy seas in open water, causing much motion on board

Sloop a single-masted sailboat with a mainsail and single jib

Stand-on vessel the vessel that has the right of way, the right to proceed unhindered by another vessel; also called the PRIVILEGED VESSEL

Starboard the right side of the vessel, when facing the BOW

Starboard tack the TACK where the wind crosses the STARBOARD side first. The sailboat on the starboard tack is the PRIVILEGED (stand-on) VESSEL.

Stern the back end of the vessel

Storm Force 10 on the BEAUFORT SCALE, with winds from 48 to 63 KNOTs (55-72 MPH)

Swallow-tail a flag having a divided end in the shape of a bird's tail

Tack (1) to change course in a zigzag manner while sailing upwind. (2) a change in course.

Tide the vertical rise and fall of water caused by the gravitational pull of the moon and sun

Topsides the sides of the hull above the waterline

Trawler a popular type of powerboat with the characteristics of slow, steady speed, comfortable living quarters, and long range under power

Truck the wooden circular cap on a traditional mast

Tuna tower a metal armature rising above the BRIDGE on a sportfishing boat, with a small platform for an observer to stand and scout out fish

Two-blocked hauled all the way up so the two parts meet and cannot go any further

Under way in motion through the water

Union the CANTON of the American flag: the blue field with fifty white stars

Union Jack the blue flag with fifty white stars flown from the BOW on Sundays, at anchor, from 8 A.M. to sunset

VHF radio *very high frequency* radiotelephone with a maximum range of about 25 miles

Warps, **streaming** dragging heavy LINEs to slow a boat in STORM conditions

Watch captain the person designated by the skipper as the one in charge of the vessel's safety during a specified time, his or her *watch*

Way the movement of a ship through the water, using her own power

Windward side the side the wind reaches first

Yacht a boat designed for pleasure rather than commerce, fishing, or work; one that has amenities suggesting luxury and comfort

Yacht ensign the optional flag flown in place of the U.S. ENSIGN by documented yachts in domestic waters

Yawl a two-masted vessel on which the MIZZEN is small and is stepped aft of the rudderpost

INDEX

INTERNATIONAL FL

Alfa
Diver Down;
Keep Clear

Kilo
Desire to Communicate

Bravo
Dangerous Cargo

Lima
Stop Instantly

Charlie
Yes

Mike
I Am Stopped

Delta
Keep Clear

November
No

Echo
Altering Course to
Starboard

Oscar
Man Overboard

Foxtrot
Disabled

Papa
About to Sail

Golf
Want a Pilot

Quebec
Request Pratique

Hotel
Pilot on Board

Romeo

India
Altering Course to Port

Sierra
Engines Going Astern

Juliett
On Fire; Keep Clear

Tango
Keep Clear of Me